BEING
ABRAHAM

GROWING OLD WITH GOD

pg - 58,

Jessie Coates

Outskirts Press, Inc.
Denver, Colorado

Outskirts Press, Inc.
http://www.outskirtspress.com

ISBN -978-1-4327-1699-8

Outskirts Press and the "OP" logo are trademarks belonging to Outskirts Press, Inc.

PRINTED IN THE UNITED STATES OF AMERICA

In memory of my beloved husband David.

This book is dedicated to his four sons,
Paul, Philip, Karl and David, and their families.

Contents

Introduction

Why would I liken you and myself to Abraham? Isn't that the most far-out notion? I might just as well liken you to the Apostle Paul or King David. Well, yes, that could be done too. They were people, ordinary people, who became special because God got involved in their lives. Now that does describe you, doesn't it?

If you're reading a book about growing old with God, you obviously know something about God, so that's O.K; I don't need to apologize for that. But you may have doubts about whether you're chosen. Abraham was chosen, but you're not sure you are. It seems rather conceited to imagine God would choose you over everyone else. Yes, it would be conceited, but that's not what happened. God didn't choose you over everyone else. He chose the whole human race, as his friends, family and worshippers. We say we are chosen because it was God's idea before it became our idea.

Abraham is such a highly revered person, such a wonderful person, that to suggest you and he are even remotely alike seems overwhelmingly conceited. But, actually, Abraham's chief virtue was that he trusted and obeyed God. God did the molding and the making. If you are trusting God and obeying him, then you can compare your life to Abraham's.

Chapter 1

GROWING OLD WITH GOD
Abraham was old and well advanced in years

I was shopping with my sixty-five year old grandma when she bought herself a new pair of shoes. Handing over the money she whispered to me, "This is the last pair of shoes I'll ever need. I won't live much longer." Over the next eighteen years my grandma repeated that phrase countless times and it became a family joke. Grandma lived to be eighty-three but it was a surprise to her. She had never intended to be old. Her son was killed in the war and she was sure she would die of sorrow, but she didn't. Her second husband died of cancer and she wanted to die too, but she didn't.

So what do we, the septuagenarians and the octogenarians, do with life when it lasts longer than we planned? Abraham and Sarah seemed to be role models for growing old, so I read their stories again and realized I had found the perfect plan for growing old. They had a reason for living. Abraham and Sarah were called to be blessed and be a blessing. Now this is something old people don't have to work too hard at, because God will do the blessing (this has always been his desire) and blessings have this way of just naturally overflowing to other people.

When I was young, churches sang a song called. 'Count Your Blessings', but I didn't want to count them; I wanted to get them. My concept of a blessing at that time was either to realize my ambitions or to acquire some needed possessions.

I had to be old in order to have time to survey my past and suddenly I saw it: countless blessings, in every shape and form. My life was strewn with blessings like a rose bed in autumn is strewn with petals.

God was starting a great work when he called Abraham. He was finding a man, and then a family, and then a nation to whom he could tell secrets. The secrets would begin to restore the broken union between God and humanity. But, first, humanity needed to know who God was and what was his nature. God has many ways of speaking to humanity. When he called Abraham, he was planning to reveal himself through his involvement in the lives of Abraham and Sarah. A similar thing happens in our present-day lives. The life-story of any faithful follower of God reveals the nature of God, it is shown in the way he preserves, leads and blesses an individual. Through this individual's life-story the following generation gets a glimpse of what God is like and how we can have unity with him.

The great records kept for all generations have been collated and preserved for us in the Bible, but individuals who have not yet begun to consciously unite with God have little interest in that great collection; they find it perplexing. They do, however, enjoy and learn from the life stories of their own relatives, especially those relatives whose lives evidence a lifetime of trusting God. For this reason I have included some of my own stories in this book, also in the hope that other grandparents who read this book will add some written stories to the collection of photographs that they are keeping to pass on to their younger relatives.

The things Abraham learned about God are no longer secrets but they are hidden: hidden from people who have not learned how to see the presence of the divine in the midst of the mundane ordinary world.

A young woman sometimes attended Van Brunt Church in Kansas City. It was a small congregation and I knew everyone in it, except this young woman. She came about once every three months, always sat in the same seat and left before the last hymn was sung. One day I got a chance to speak to her. After I'd told her how glad I was to see her, she told me that when she was a little girl she used to come to this church with her grandmother, who had since died. Whenever the stress in her life got too great, she felt drawn to come back to the church and sit in the same place she used to sit with her grandmother. Whenever she did this, a great peace came over her and she felt strong again. That grandma was like Abraham and Sarah; she passed a spiritual inheritance to her grandchild.

The promise of blessing and being a blessing was given to Abraham and then passed on to his children. The true inheritance was faith. But note this: it was not Abraham's faith they inherited, because everyone must believe for themselves, but it was God's faith-keeping that was given to them, the faithfulness of God. "God is faithful." That phrase repeats itself constantly as we look over our lives. God will keep every promise he has made and when we leave this life he will still be answering the prayers we prayed for our loved ones. He will still be watching over them as they make their journey through the increasing complexities of civilization in a world we can only wonder about.

Chapter 2

YOU HEARD WHAT?
God said

Some people hear it early in life; other people think they never heard it. What is it? The voice of God. Abraham heard it early in life. He heard God say, "Go to a place which I will show you." How did he know it was the voice of God? The difficulty lies not in hearing the voice but in recognizing it. God spoke this earth into order when it was bathed in chaos. God spoke and it was so. But the word God speaks to people is not one of command but invitation. How do we recognize it among all the other voices in this world? Watching the life and blessings of Abraham, was one way the desert nations heard God speak. Abraham's life spoke of a covenant, an agreement entered into with God and signed with flesh. His life gave evidence of God's patience, preservation and blessing. This was the message that God spoke through the life of Abraham and Sarah. It was not the man himself that was the message, but God's very evident care for him.

Some people looked at the evidence and understood that Abraham's God was truly God, living and powerful. Every-

the other side of the mountain. He woke to find that it was a couple hours later, and there was more weather from the northeast, with waves breaking over the rail and washing across the pile of fish on deck. The fish had been packed tightly against the scuppers so the *Desire* could not clear her decks and was gaining more weight from seawater. It was dark, and the lights of Ocean City sparkled in the night. Mordecai rubbed his eyes, and Wolf told him to take the watch; that he was going below to check on the pumps and see if water was coming into the boat. On the radar, Mordecai saw three blips coming toward the stern rapidly from the east. By the speed of their approach, he knew it was the three fiberglass Brunos. As the boats approached the inlet, two of them came up alongside the *Desire*, and Mordecai heard the rumble of their diesels and saw the silhouettes of the men in the wheelhouse. Instead of just blasting ahead, Mordecai heard the pitch of their motors change as two throttled down and slipped ahead. The inlet was completely awash with surf and white foam. They would be entering in a following sea. With their powerful lights illuminating the water in front of them, the Brunos lined up in front of the inlet and stopped just outside. Mordecai could hear their conversation over the radio.

"You gonna go first, Jan?"

"Yeah, here goes nothing."

A giant swell approached the stern of the two boats. As it lifted and passed beneath them, one gunned its motor and took off, full throttle, right behind the wave, and crossed the inlet between giant swells that, if they had caught the tiny craft, would have smashed it onto the shoals. The third Bruno cruised just astern of *Desire*. With the next swell, the second Bruno copied the first and slipped through the inlet and into Ocean City Harbor. Wolf came up from below and muttered something about the stuffing box leaking and the lazarette having water in it. Mordecai mentioned the technique he had just witnessed the Brunos use to enter the harbor; the third was hanging back a little more. Mordecai stepped out onto the deck, Wolf headed for the center of the inlet. The *Desire* entered the churning foam, and the boat was lifted on a great swell as it entered the inlet, right in the middle of its northern and southern edges. The wave passed under, and the boat slid down its back. With a slam, the *Desire* felt like it had been

one saw the evidence, but not everyone heard the message.

The voice of God can come through our lives also. We need not hide the great and good things that happened to us, for they are the visible blessings of God. But when we tell the happy parts of our lives, the message that we want to speak through our story is not how good we were, but how faithful God is.

Very few of my congregation heard a sound but many of them heard words. The words formed in their understanding, sometimes quickly and instantaneously, other times over a long time of thought and reflection. When they stood in front of the congregation and declared their desire to join the church, they had all arrived at the same conclusion, that Jesus Christ was their Lord and Savior, that they trusted him, and intended to follow him. They had all heard the voice.

When I worked as a hospital chaplain, I talked with people who heard voices. The difference with the voices they heard and the voice of God was that they were afraid of the voices, terrified of what the voices told them to do. When they shared with other people what the voices said the other people had no trouble saying that the voices were false. People do hear their thoughts so loudly that they sound like voices. The brain does sometimes play back words from a person's memory. But these voices are not consistent in their message. If the message is harmful it is not the voice of God. If the message is destructive, it is coming from another source.

Of all the people I asked about their recognition of the message of God, one lady told me the youngest story I have yet heard. She lived on a farmstead, and one day, when she was four years old, she was told to go across the farmyard to the farm dairy and bring back something her mother needed. Looking out into the darkness of the evening and the shadows in the yard she said, "I dare not go into the darkness."

"God will go with you," her mother answered. The woman who told me this story knows that her mother's words were words from God because to this day she has never felt afraid and is still aware of the presence of God with her. She recognized the word of God in words she heard from her mother.

The Apostle Paul saw a brilliant light and heard a voice. The Apostle Peter met a man he had probably seen in the local synagogue. The man issued an invitation, and he accepted the invitation before he was completely convinced of the identity of the speaker. During the following two to three years, he listened often to the voice of God speaking through the words of Jesus. Through the teaching, through the healing, he came at last to a strong conviction. "You are the Son of God," he said to Jesus. There were people in my churches who were going this slow route. Not many of them had had anything like Paul's experience. But listening to the record of the words of Jesus, reading the Old Testament record of the actions of God, calling out to God when they needed a job or a healing, slowly they came to a decision. They had listened a long time before they recognized the voice. When they did, they often understood the urgency of showing respect for the words of God spoken to the children of man. They came on strongly in the faith, filled at last with a recognition of what they had been hearing – the voice of God.

I want to make a suggestion: that you begin to write down all the times you believe God brought something to your attention that led you to do something you are glad about now. It is my guess that as you write you will remember more and recognize more. You will be amazed because God has been with you, as he was with Abraham.

Chapter 3

STARTING OUT
Go from your country and your people

When David and I loaded our little boys, aged just 4 and almost 2 and drove away from that little chapel building in the back streets of Leeds, we and all our family and friends were mindful of Abraham's leaving behind the place where he had lived and his relatives. We were eager to go because we wanted to spread the news of blessing. We wanted to tell people living in Japan that God's intention for humanity was to bless them, and make them a blessing.

We were going to tell the promise that God made to Abraham, and hoped to tell it to many who had never heard. We were acutely aware that we were joining a long procession of promise bearers.

My father had prayed that nothing bad would happen to us on our journey to London. On the way (on the old A1 road) the car stopped suddenly and violently. The motor cyclists behind us had no time to stop and pitched into the car at speed. No one was hurt. I forget all the details about getting the car repaired on a Sunday, but I remember the explanation: the brakes had simply seized up because the car was brand new, and new cars sometimes did seize up until all the parts had settled down. (This was 1954, and our car was the least expensive kind that Ford made.) When we spoke by phone to my father, he was bewildered. "But I prayed that nothing would happen to you," he said.

Father knew very well that bad things happen to people who are trying to serve God. He said no more but I think (to use Biblical language) that he was being warned by God. God was in fact saying, "Don't expect this journey of theirs to be easy, glorious, or even successful." Father never got ashamed or exasperated because we did not write home about mighty miracles and earth-shaking successes; everyone else did. They were sending "all that money" (actually it was ridiculously little) to replicate the success that missionaries in the heart of Africa were having, but we only wrote home with apologetic stories of little groups and small beginnings.

So, I wonder, did Abraham have difficulties when his band of people set out to go to a place that God had told them to go to? Or was it all simple? He traveled a route that bordered the Mediterranean Sea. There were other families also making the emigration journey from Haran and from Ur. The route was fairly simple, traveled by merchants carrying imported goods: about 17 miles each day from one small settlement to another. No visible angels attended his way, and no celestial lights lit up when he reached Shecham and knew he had arrived.

Chapter 4

NO WELCOME BAND, NO TICKER TAPE PARADE

They came into the land of Canaan

There is a comfort in being able to say, "I did what God wanted me to do." But there is also often a sense of anti-climax. What do I do next? Abraham was to live in that country of Canaan, traveling from pasture land to pasture land, still trusting the God who spoke to him, and to become a blessing to all those around him. He was to continue the spiritual journey that had started with a geographical journey. His spiritual journey consisted of believing in God and doing what he knew God wanted him to do. You and I are called to that same journey. Life is a spiritual pilgrimage, even if we never leave the town where we were born.

In this area in particular we may feel we have something in common with Abraham: nothing happened when he got there. The local inhabitants did not rush out to greet him; water did not spring out of the ground. When you and I look at our lives we often have the same feeling: we haven't done anything different to what countless other people did. We haven't achieved any great purpose.

God had promised to give Abraham the land he had arrived at, but it did not become his. God had promised to make his name great, but he was just a rich nomad, his wife was still barren, and famines and kings continued to threaten his existence. Abraham's journey to Canaan had been made. Did he sometimes look up to the sky in bewilderment and ask, "Is this all you want me to do, God?" He lived his life traveling around the country he had journeyed to, feeding his flocks and serving the One God and waiting, waiting, waiting, for God to keep the promise he had made to him.

So how does this apply to us today? We have made the spiritual journey we felt called to make and arrived at a state of commitment and obedience to the One God, but nothing else seems to have happened. Our lives continue, changed from before, but no wonderful climax presents itself to us. We are inheritors of the promise made to Abraham but it seems that for a while all that is required of us is to continue to believe in God and carry on acting the way he wants us to.

While we are moving around in geography, another kind of journey is happening inside us: a spiritual journey. As we share our life with God, that life becomes a pilgrimage, an inner journey, with landmarks and characteristics that we remember but are not visible to anyone else. We journey in faith towards a promised future and the journey becomes a fantastic adventure of conversation with God, decisions made with him, actions done in his name and eventually praise that comes naturally and is happily directed toward the God of Promise. In a small way, we are being Abraham.

Abraham arrived in Canaan, and he was one man accompanied by his wife, his nephew and what we would call his household staff. He had probably lived in houses before.

The houses in Ur were set in streets. They had tiled floors, and waste water flowed down drains in the street. Now he lived in tents. He may have been a merchant in the past but now he was just a cattle breeder. From that one man were to come two nations, both innumerable, plus all the spiritual descendants who were not Jews by birth but born of God by the will of God. You would have thought, wouldn't you, that if God intended to do something that big, then he would at least have started with a group of people.

There's a legend that one man, Joseph of Arimathea, and his companions came to England to bring the good news of Jesus. They disembarked at Glastonbury in Somerset, and began the steep climb up the cliff. They rested on the way, at a place called Weary-all Hill. From the spot where they are believed to have rested you can see the land stretching far out into the distance. What an impossible task: just a few people trying to bring the good news to a whole country. But Christianity flourished in England, reviving again and again after successive invasions by people who served tribal gods. Every town in Britain has a church as well as several Christian meeting houses and chapels.

We, the older Christians, have reason to be optimistic about our lives. The results of God's blessing on Abraham were effective long after Abraham died, and still continue. We do not know what consequences have come from acts of kindness or self-sacrifice done because we believed God called us to do so.

"Abraham was only one person when I called him," says God through the prophet Isaiah, "But when I blessed him, he became a great nation." Then Isaiah adds, "The Lord will bless Israel again, and make her deserts blossom" What you and I have to consider is not how to try and make Christianity powerful and popular. The only thing we have to ask ourselves is: are we believing the promises of God and are we living faithfully so that God may bless us, and our descendants after us, and their descendants also? We have much to think about and a lot of people born and unborn to pray about.

Chapter 5

GOD BLESS YOU
I will bless you and make you a blessing

God bless you! If you want to hear those words just give two quarters to the next person standing on the sidewalk, asking for money. That homeless penniless person has just prayed for you the most comprehensive prayer known to humanity. The Almighty has been asked to do you a favor, and it is very likely he will. This does not mean that you can buy the favor of Almighty; it only means that God answers prayers, especially unselfish ones.

What is this word 'bless' that we hear so often, and use so often. It means much more than happy. Somewhere around three millennia ago, God instructed Moses to tell the chief priest to put God's name on the children of Israel by blessing them. The blessing involved three activities of God.

- ☐ God preserving them from harm and danger;
- ☐ God seeing them and being gracious to them;
- ☐ God giving enlightenment and peaceful security to them.

This is a what God intended to do when he said he would bless Abraham and make him a blessing to all the nations of the world.

It always comes as a surprise to me that before God blessed the people he had caused to exist, he first blessed the fish and birds. My generation tended to think that everything on earth was there for two reasons: either to be used or to be eaten.

Riding the bus from Moortown into the center of Leeds city, I was glad to find an empty seat. I was about eight months pregnant and felt a little guilty about inconveniencing the three or four men who all stood up as soon as I boarded the bus and offered me their seat. I took the nearest offer and sat down next to a man whose clothes informed me that he was a Rabbi. After a little while he leaned over to me and said, "Do you know what is the first commandment ever given?"

"Be fruitful and multiply" I replied.

"Oh, I'm surprised. I didn't think you'd know that."

In the early days, when there was an abundance of food and space on the earth, God frequently blessed the earth and the people with the words, "Be fruitful and multiply".

With me in the elevator one day was a woman and small child. We were in a hospital riding up to the children's ward on the fourth floor. The child was wearing pajamas and was obviously a patient who had been allowed the only great adventure that patients can have – a trip to the gift shop. I had come from a funeral and was still wearing a clerical collar. Suddenly the little girl was pushed towards me and the woman demanded in an urgent way, "Bless her, Sister, bless her now, before she goes back into that room." I didn't stop to explain the mistaken identity but did what any Sister friend of mine would have done. I put my hand on the child's head, asked God to bless her with good health and salvation. The woman thanked me so heartily that her faith in God was evident and I'm quite sure he heard and answered that hasty prayer in an elevator.

What did it mean to Abraham when God said he would bless him and make him a blessing? What does it mean to you and me that God is eager to bless us and make us a blessing? Well, because we are old it means much more to us than it would have done when we were confident young people. Now that we are older, our friends and relatives are fewer and we meet only a few new people. We fear being a burden and rarely think of ourselves as a blessing. Perhaps you are like me, still overwhelmed by sorrow because my husband is not here, feeling the geographical distance between my old friends and my new address, missing the days when I was a pastor and part of a busy group of people. In spite of these things I remind myself that God wants to bless all people, and he wants everyone to be a blessing to somebody else. It is true that the Greek word for blessing, 'makarios', is understood to mean 'happy' but it is a shallow understanding of a profound truth. To be blessed by God is to have him involved with your life (whether you recognize it or not). Happiness is fleeting; blessings remain when happiness has gone.

God blessed Abraham in a visible way. Abraham became rich. And because he was rich and had many household servants, he became powerful. The surrounding tribes in the desert were worshipping nature and fertility gods. The only way they had of choosing between the supposed deities was by whichever one appeared to have granted them rain and good crops. They had no way of understanding the concept of One God, and perhaps they felt that this narrowed down their options. They needed a simple visible demonstration of the power of Abraham's One God, the one they often referred to as the most high [or tallest] God. Most especially they feared angering the nature gods. They needed a demonstration of the benevolence of God. Abraham's prospering gave evidence of God's activity in his life, and showed that God was for us.

So, a blessing may take many shapes but it should give evidence to surrounding people that God is with us and for us. Sometimes when Abraham was about to spoil the whole joint venture between him and God, God thwarted him. Even the frustrations of life can be blessings in disguise.

"Blessing" means much more than "Long life, health and prosperity". That definition would omit many of the ways in which God plans to show us favor. That is what blessing is – it is God giving us favors, not because we deserve them but because this is what he intends to do.

Since showing favors is the very nature of God, who can stop him? We can; by avoiding him, distrusting him, by insulting him. When we have a right attitude towards him, as Abraham did, when we are so trustful of him that we seek to bring our conduct into line with his instructions, then we have made ourselves available to the innumerable favors that God grants.

My Aunt Winifred was the last of three parents (that's including the step-dad) and four siblings. Osteomylitis had devoured her bones and she told me that the doctor had described her spine as 'turning into chalk'. In the last five years of her life she was unable to walk. She sat up in her bed and watched television, read the newspaper and talked on the phone. This was her life and she felt useless.

She lived in England where the local doctor made house visits. One day, when the doctor visited her, Aunt Win asked him if there was any way she could hasten her death because she was a burden to her country. The visiting doctor sat down on her bed and explained something to her.

He said, "I come from India. I and my parents worked very hard so I could get through medical school. My parents gave me everything they had and when I finished medical school they had no money left.. I came to England to work because now I have to support my parents and I need more money than I can get in India. Whenever I come to visit you the National Health Office pays me a little money. I send as much as I can to my parents to care for them in their old age. To me you are not a burden but a blessing."

The National Health Service provided a home care-giver who visited Aunt Win every day; gave her breakfast, made her bed, cleaned her room and cooked two more meals which were left on a tray by her bedside. When I visited Aunt Win the care-giver told me, "I have two other patients. They grumble and weep and think I am their slave. Whenever I visit your Aunt she welcomes me, and speaks kindly. She has asked that my children sometimes visit her and is as proud of them as if they were her own children. My life is difficult just now and I feel that no one really cares about me, except your aunt. She takes a personal interest and prays for me at night. I don't know what I would do without her."

I think my Aunt Win regarded her invalid years as a kind of pilgrimage. She had been walking with God when her spine deteriorated. She faced a journey into helplessness that was frightening. Like Abraham, she journeyed in faith. Like Abraham, she had a promise to sustain her: the end of her journey would bring her to God himself and the realization of every good hope. In her own time and place, she was being Abraham.

Chapter 6

SEEING GOD
God appeared to Abraham and said…

There was a member of one of my churches who was blind. Blindness had come upon her late in life and so she hadn't learnt Braille and was too old to risk falling and breaking a bone, so she stayed in her home, listening to the radio. She had a live-in housekeeper. Members of our church visited her often. She had been an active member before she lost her sight. The friends kept her up to date with news of the events in the congregation and she was mentally very bright. I used to take communion to her once a month. We always invited the housekeeper, whom I'm going to call Violet, to take communion; she always refused, but said she would like to listen to the prayers.

Since Mrs. Grey didn't need someone with her continually, I suggested that Violet might like to come to a Sunday morning service at our church. Violet replied, "Oh no, I could never do that that."

"Why not?" I asked. In a matter of fact way, Violet replied that she was a wicked woman. "Makes no difference," I replied. "Church is for sinners."

Violet looked at me strangely, and paused for emphasis. "Pastor, I mean wicked." Now that was an opportunity to get all theological about the fact that we are all sinners, but I sensed Violet was trying to tell me something so I just kept quiet. "I used to be young, and beautiful; that kind of wicked," said Violet.

"Well there's a few of that kind of wicked in the Bible," I said, "so why not come to church?"

"I can't," said Violet. "Most of the women in that church wouldn't sit at a table with me, least of all share a church pew." I knew that was true. The church I was serving at that time was an old, well-established congregation. Most of the people attending were the widows of professional men. One of the problems with that kind of congregation is that they tend to confuse respectability with righteousness. Most of them just can't tell the difference.

"But she's good now," said Mrs. Grey. "She's been good to me, so I'm sure God's forgiven her." My evangelistic friends would wonder why I didn't start preaching that minute and put them both right, but I have kind of noticed that when a person is making their way towards God, it's not always helpful to rush them. Besides, I needed to do some converting of Christians.

It did cross my mind that if Mrs. Grey died Violet would be left without friends and perhaps without money. But unexpectedly it was Violet who died first. Her cancer was advanced and she was no longer able to bear the pain when she finally went to see the doctor. I visited her in hospital and prayed for her. She thanked me. I went three days later, and she couldn't wait till the greetings were over before she said, "Sit down. I've something I want you to know. Last night I couldn't sleep for pain but I looked up from my pillow and there was Jesus standing at the foot of my bed. He was smiling at me."

Of course I believed her. Didn't Jesus speak to me when I was just a six-and-a-half year-old child? Hadn't I listened to story after story about Jesus speaking to people and people seeing the Holy City on the night before they died? Those things were consistent with her statement that Jesus appeared to her. "Do you think you'll see Jesus again?" I asked, and she knew what I meant.

"Oh yes, I'll see him in heaven." she said.

Now it was time to help her get through the door, now that she'd been welcomed. So I asked her, "Violet are you going to heaven because you've been good to Mrs. Grey?" She looked at me and replied, "I'm going to heaven because Jesus died for my sins." She was through the door, safe home. If I'd been an emotional person I'd have cried for joy, but in those days I was fervent and eager. I rarely stopped to give thanks and was always struggling to do the next good thing.

Why did God appear to Abraham? Was it because he'd been good and obeyed God by making the journey from Haran to Canaan? Or was it because God gives favors to people simply because he is good and it's his nature to bless everyone who will let him get near them?

Chapter 7

GETTING CONNECTED TO GOD
There he built an altar

It is a long time since I read the book written by Svetlana, Stalin's daughter, but I remember that while she was being raised in a country where all knowledge of God was suppressed she privately believed that the moon was God, and would sit by her bedroom window and gaze at what she thought was God made visible.

The people in the towns where Abraham had come from believed the same thing. They built huge temples to the god Sin and worshiped the stars in the sky. Their gods were visible; they did not have to argue about their existence. Abraham's God was invisible.

The first recorded act of Abraham after he arrived in the place he'd been told to go to was to build an altar. The temples to the moon god Sin, were huge and impressive but Abraham never built a temple. He built altars; four of them that we know about. The altars were low platforms of gathered stones. The platform needed to be quite big, big enough to lead a large animal onto it so it could be slaughtered. A large fire was built on the platform so the animal could be burnt and the smoke could go up into the sky as a signal to God that someone on earth was worshiping him. It's unlikely that this was a private ceremony so the altar had to be big enough for all Abraham's household staff to stand round it and watch the offering being made. It was the practice of the time that the head of the household should also be the priest to the family. His prayers would state why the offering was being made: whether it was for praise, thanksgiving, supplication or repentance. The altars would be considered sacred by other travelers and would not be dismantled. It's possible that travelers would ask which god the altar was built for and would be told by anyone who knew that it was built to the Most High God, or perhaps to the Only God. How irritated other people would be at the suggestion that if Abraham's God was the only God then their god was not a god.

We who are Abraham's spiritual descendants no longer offer burnt offerings because Jesus has made one offering for all time, but we worship the same One God. Worship is our way of making contact with God. Like Abraham, we mark all the stages of our life's journey with acts of worship. We travel, says the writer of Hebrews, towards a city: the City Of God where he will be both light and environment, and all his desires for his dearly loved children will have become reality. Even when we arrive at the City of God we will still be offering worship. Then worship will be even more natural because we shall truly understand who God is, and what he has accomplished. Abraham will be there and all the generations will have become one generation. It seems a long journey, and we travel through some dry places but God who called us to begin the journey will be watching our progress.

There is a story attached to the Presbyterian Church in White Oak, Iowa. One Saturday three brothers went into a town some distance from where they lived. They went because they were farmers who lived in the fields all week and liked a change on Saturday. They went looking for company and novelty. Novelty presented itself in the shape of a tent-meeting, the three brothers went in and got converted. The next day they brought their two other brothers and they got converted too. Since it wasn't possible to travel back to that town regularly they built a small, wooden, one-room church close to their own town and called a preacher to come and lead them in worship.

The history of these little wooden churches in rural areas of America is fascinating. Buildings have been put on rollers, hitched to horses and turned round to face away from the wind, or towards the road, or some other direction. The building has been put on jacks and held up whilst a base-ment was built underneath. Ramps have been built up and towers taken down. Church bells hang at waist level in little metal frames. But worship goes on: one hundred years, one hundred and fifty... Reading the newsletters from several of those churches in Iowa I still recognize family names, but these are the sons and daughters of the people that David and I preached to. Throughout the world, from continent to continent, and from day to day people pray, people preach. The worship of God does not and will not end.

Worship is something that everyone does. It is not always directed to God but the nature of man is to worship some-thing. Sometimes it is the state, sometimes an ideology, sometimes a person. The fervency with which we love and admire something is a form of worship. The most important thing in our life, whether it be wife, children or career; be-cause it is the most important thing, becomes a focus of wor-ship.

It was dusk in the St. Louis ghetto. I was alone with my five - year old in the old mansion that was being used for a Teen Challenge Center. David phoned to say that a young man was on his way to join the program and would I please admit him. Only two weeks in America and brand new to Teen Challenge, I didn't know what was expected of me and the hasty explanation was that I had to help the young man recognize his own helplessness and God's willingness to help him. All the Teen Challenge staff including both Brent the director and David the other director were at a church somewhere leading a service and would be home very late

The young man came. Over a cup of coffee he made it fairly easy for me to 'admit' him, by telling me that he was addicted and had been trying to kick the habit without any success. Someone had told him that if he came to Teen Challenge he could get off the habit. He concluded by asking me how we got people off. I explained that we didn't but God did. "He helps people who call on him for help. Would you like to ask God to help you get off drugs now?" I asked in my still strong English accent and refined manner of speech. "Just talk to God in your own words."

"Hey Man, I've got this habit and I want to kick it, and I've tried but it's got a hold of me. This woman, she says, you can do something for me, so please, get me off if you can."

I was shocked. Calling God 'Man' was denying his deity: that was blasphemy. The whole prayer lacked any sort of reverence. In Japan I'd heard God called 'Kami sama'; in England we addressed God with many respectful adjectives before his name. I hastily 'backed up' the young man's prayer by appealing to God by name and addressing him with reverence.

When the staff of Teen Challenge returned from the meeting they'd been leading they explained to me that 'The Man' was the name for an authority figure and that actually the title was quite respectful, for someone who didn't know any other name for God.

Abraham built at altar when he reached the place he was

called to go to. Later he built another altar, further south. This time, the record says that he called on the name of the Lord. He wasn't the first man to do so. After Cain killed Abel, there appears to have been a great silence on earth, until Enosh was born. "Then", says the Bible, "men began to call on the name of the Lord." 'Call' meant as many things in Hebrew as it does in English: calling out to address someone, praise them or request help were some of the meanings.

So, the inclusion of the words 'called upon the name of the Lord,' at the second altar but not the first, may indicate progress in the relationship between Abraham and the Lord. We older people know about that. Over many years we've proved that God is kind to all who call upon him and so we call more often now, and with more confidence. Abraham was threatened by famine and hostility; we are threatened by many circumstances. Like Abraham we know that we are invited to call upon God for help. Perhaps Abraham had another reason for praying; was he ever lonely? He belonged to no local tribe, the language was different where he was to where he came from, and he had no sons to make plans with. Many older people are lonely; their family is far away, they do not live where they grew up, they miss old friends. Abraham called upon the name of the Lord, and God was with him. I have proved that so many times, so many ways, since I was left a widow. Other widows call me up and tell me with excitement, how God helped them make decisions or pointed them in a certain direction. The God of Abraham is our God and his kindness is to us, and for us, forever. It is natural to miss other company of our own age and background, but the God who travels with us will lessen the loneliness

Chapter 8

DISAPPOINTMENT
There was a famine in the land

Abraham had done what God directed him to do. He had left his family and his father's house and gone to the place God showed him. And what happened?. Nothing! Sarah did not get pregnant, he didn't own any single patch of ground and after a time the land itself stopped producing and there was famine in the very place he had been told to come to.

So Abraham left the land he'd been told to go to. He went traveling on to Egypt. We know the end of the story but Abraham didn't. What did Abraham think as he journeyed away from the place he had journeyed to? We know Abraham believed God; scripture emphasizes that. Was his faith mixed with disappointment that day, as he left the land behind and journeyed towards Egypt? We are told that he was apprehensive as he entered yet another strange country. He was afraid he would be killed and was thinking he would perhaps give away this woman who was his unproductive wife.

How does this apply to us? It certainly applies to everyone

who has tried to live a life of service to humanity, because very often many of us are bewildered and disappointed.

Let me tell you about the disappointment. It is part of the reason I have chosen to think and write about Abraham: to encourage myself. The best sermon a pastor can preach is the one he or she preaches to himself or herself, so don't think it selfish of me to write about myself.

There has been a purpose in my life since the time I was six and half. It became a passion that possessed me, and it has been moderately fulfilled, but not wonderfully fulfilled

When I was six and a half I returned home from the service where I had become aware of Christ's friendship. While my parents bustled about seeing to fires and food I went into the dining room alone and addressed the presence I had felt in church. "What a lot of happiness," I said, talking about myself. A thought came into my mind with a clarity that caused me to know God had spoken to me. "There are a lot of unhappy people in this world. You must tell them about me so they can have the same happiness you have." From that day on I talked of Jesus, and began preaching when I was 13 years old. In my teen years a picture was always in my mind. It was of the father of the prodigal son standing by his house looking down the road longing for his absent son to return. I began to understand that God suffers. I began to feel his pain and I became passionate and driven by my desire to tell people about Jesus.

David and I gave our possessions, our time and energy to help bring God's absentee children back to unite with God their Father, who longs to make them happy. We had many moderate successes, but the numbers who responded were not the numbers we prayed for. For that reason we both experienced disappointment. We opened one new church, assisted three that were already open, and worked in partnership with a student who had opened a church without sponsorship. We taught Bible School, gave hospitality, held classes, and were disappointed with ourselves because we felt we had accomplished so little. That is why I wonder if Abraham ever felt disappointment. I think of the promise God made to Abraham that he would have descendants as innumerable as the stars, and I contrast that with the fact that when Abraham was a hundred his wife gave birth to one son. Just one.

Our sons have been a great help, reminding us of the integrity with which David served. The disappointment has lessened and I begin to entertain a lot of hope. Because although the results of our labors (and I mean labors) were small compared to what some other people have had; perhaps in the same way that God gave Abraham millions of descendants from only one son maybe the results of our labors will be more than we realize. David was content to do his best and leave the rest to God. I never was. I prayed and prayed to be made more effective and wept with disappointment because I wasn't.

There may be other people out there who feel a similar disappointment about their own lives: hopes that weren't realized, and dreams that didn't come true. So I encourage myself and I encourage them. God kept on keeping his promise to Abraham through Abraham's descendants, and through their descendants. God hears and answers our prayers and is faithful to the promises he makes. We haven't seen the end of the story yet.

Chapter 9

SELLING SARAH

Say you are my sister, so that I may stay alive

Suddenly we don't know Abraham anymore. He is no longer the adventurous traveler following divine direction. Throughout scripture Abraham is commended because he believed the promise God gave him, in spite of the fact that twice scripture says he was willing to sell his wife to save his life. Sarah was his half-sister, daughter of his father by a different mother, and way back when there were fewer people, there was no shame in marrying your half-sister. This woman, ten biblical years younger than himself and strikingly beautiful, had grown up in the same household as Abraham. She shared his memories and knew the names of his relatives. He asked her to do him a favor and not tell anyone they were married in case he was killed and his wife treated as the spoils of war.

Famine behind him, danger before him: who can blame Abraham for arriving at a deception that afforded both of them relative safety. The romantically inclined among us would prefer Abraham to have declared that he would die rather than loose his wife, but a woman without male protection would be at the mercy of everybody, whereas a woman whose brother was a cattle herder traveling with his household staff was in a much safer position.

It happened as Abraham had expected. Perhaps he had not expected that the man who would want Sarah (or Sarai as she was then called) would be the Pharaoh of Egypt, but it was to Pharaoh's harem that she was taken. Pharaoh bought Sarah by paying Abraham with much livestock and many servants.

God intervened. He plagued Pharaoh's household with great plagues and Pharaoh learned that the woman Sarah was actually the wife of Abraham. Pharaoh believed himself badly treated and lied to. He sent Sarah and Abraham away, saying something equivalent to, 'Take her and go away.'

Abraham left, taking with him the payment he had received. In Pharaoh's eyes, Abraham must have appeared as a scheming liar.

The action detracted from God's reputation because although he rescued Sarah, the two people who were meant to be a demonstration of God's love and kindness now left the palace in disgrace.

This is a convenient sermon to preach on the Sunday when the preacher returns from vacation. He or she can preach for 20 minutes, half an hour, about the sin of deceit and draw attention to the fact that a half truth becomes a whole lie. He can get dramatic about the 'Father of Lies' and the consequence of deception. Then he can preach for another half hour about the folly of solving your own problems without waiting for God to guide you. He wouldn't need to do any research, and hardly need to quote the Bible, just talk out of his own convictions.

Teaching morals is not why the Bible was written however.

The Bible was verbally rehearsed, written down and preserved in order that we might know God. It is because we know God that we want to become moral: because God is good and no shadow of deceit is in him. Most Christians hold the same standards that were taught by their Christian parents and confirmed by reading of the Bible. But do all Christians know why? Can they explain those morals to their rebel grandchildren in an understandable way? If we are unfortunate enough to learn that our grandchildren are doing something that we totally disapprove of our initial shock and concern over-rides our efforts to talk reasonably. But maybe an emotional response is not so bad after all. It at least shows the degree of concern we feel. Our job as witnesses on behalf of God is to pass on the stories in the scriptures and use those stories as the basis for choosing morals, preferably before the time for decision arrives. For instance if someone wonders aloud if a half-truth is a lie, we can re-tell the story of Abraham's half-truth and ask the person to reach their own decision about the difference between the whole truth and suppression of half of the truth. Hopefully then, their morals will not be what they were taught but what they chose.

The Spirit of Jesus dwells in everyone who calls him Lord and Savior. It is by shaping our actions to be like his actions that we become people with standards of conduct.

What did Sarah and Abraham know about the One God? Perhaps at this stage of their great adventure they did not know a great deal about God. They had been born in Ur where the moon was god, had travelled through a region where many fertility gods were worshipped and come out the other side of that region into Egypt, where the sun was god. In each of these religions the god was feared. He needed to be placated and sometimes bribed. The inhabitants imagined their gods as being easily displeased and very vengeful.

To explain how God reacts when displeased, people often use

a very simple illustration. When one of my grandchildren misbehaves his father expresses his displeasure and sends the child to his or her room alone. My son remains in the same house and would go to them immediately if there was any danger. Although angry he still loves them. When they ask if they can come back to be with him he explains why he is angry and when they promise not to repeat the offence, they are hugged and kissed and restored to the family presence. It is possible that Abraham understood very little of this in the early stages of his journey with God. What he found out and passed on for us all to learn is that God continued to watch over him and Sarah even though they were dishonoring him. He protected them and brought them out of the palace.

Through his actions towards Abraham and Sarah God reveals who he is and how he acts towards humanity. Through this part of their life- story we learn that God is caring, loving and forgiving, as long as our earthly life continues. Only that long however; scripture gives absolutely no evidence of God forgiving someone who waited till the events of life after death compel belief. God did not abandon these two people to the consequences of a decision reached in extremity. He stayed with them and required no sacrifices to awake his compassion. This is an early example of the faithfulness of God. An early English translation calls it the "loving-kindness of God". Although they had felt helpless and afraid when they entered the mighty country of Egypt, they learnt (and probably to their surprise) that God would protect them, even in the Pharaoh's house. God did and does rescue his people from every power on earth. He turns our fear and trepidation into relief and gratitude. You and I can confidently call on the name of the Lord knowing that he hears our prayers and that he will bring us out of, or go with us in, every tribulation.

Chapter 10

GOING BACK TO THE BEGINNING

Abraham returned to where he had made the first altar.

How about you, do you ever want to return to a place in your past? Could you if you tried? Some people do. They come home after a career of traveling and excitement, carrying their trophies with them and retire in the same town where they grew up. David and I returned to Leeds, the town where we spent our youth. After a 12 year absence, we could no longer recognize the old land marks, and our old church building had been pulled down to make way for a development of nice modern houses.

Abraham returned to the place where he had been at the beginning. Beginning of what? Beginning of living with God in the land of promise. Native of Ur, resident of Haran he was, but Canaan was his home now. He had been forced to leave when famine struck, and, years later, he returns to the place where his tent was at the beginning and to the second altar he had built.

There is no mention of Abraham building altars in Egypt, or on his way through the Sinai peninsula, nor even in the

Negev. Of course, the record cannot state every detail of his life, so why then does the record mention this particular altar?

Abraham always believed God, and he believed confidently, but does even a confident faith sometimes grow listless during times of patient waiting? The journey to Egypt, the plot that failed in Egypt and the long journey back with his many possessions: had there been years when there was more patient confidence than joyful exhilaration? Now he is back to the place where he started from; when the grass was green, his wife trusted him, and the silent voice of God was the loudest sound in the land.

Is there a time in your faith journey when you heard the silent voice speak strongly, when the preached voice spoke truth that cut through the sinews of your being and your soul sprang to life in the truth, when your response was fervent as well as faithful? Was there a time when you thrilled like the strings of a plucked violin, with expectation, because you knew that God would be faithful to you, bless you and make you a blessing? Those times were a beginning for you, and you can return to them. Not the place where it happened, not the person who preached when your soul lept to life, but to the truths themselves. You can return. Places change, worship styles and ministers change; we can not find what used to be in what is now. But the truths themselves are still there and they will again illuminate you, liberate you and develop the spiritual person that you are. I am not talking about radical fundamentalism but about the basic simple truths of the faith. Sometimes it takes a journey to get back to the beginning. It is most likely that we shall have to make the journey alone, and even arrive alone; our churches are busy reaching a lost generation. But there is a way. You may find it through prayer and reflection, or in reading scripture and writing what it says to you, probably through the prayer books of the church and the faith confessions of past believers. Somewhere you will find again the foundations of the faith. The saints who went before will again become witnesses to God's mercy and remind you of the basic truths. You will find authenticity and be back where you were before too many duties and too great an effort dulled your faith and diminished your hope. We are constantly assured that our faith is based on facts and not on feelings, but the presence or absence of feeling is important to all of us.

Did Abraham feel blessed? We know he believed God, accepted the promise and looked for the fulfillment. But what about his feelings; did he sometimes plod along patiently? Or did he more often respond to God with amazement, excited expectancy and overflowing joy? Years later the book of Psalms would show us that the faithful believer experiences both ends of the spectrum of feelings.

What did did Sarah feel? Did she long for the life and bustle of Haran and Ur, for the house she used to live in? Did she so much long for a baby that she could feel nothing else?

Some people can go to church all their lives and never have a feeling of intense spiritual joy.. Other people seem to be having spiritual highs all the time; in fact, the rest of us almost long for them to become 'normal' and complain about something.

Mrs. (I shall call her Webster) was a lady brought up in the faith. She confirmed her faith in her very early teens because she did believe, but she would express bewilderment and a little disapproval whenever anyone told her they felt blessed. In conversation with me and sometimes in the Women's Association she talked about her faith. She said she believed in Christ because her parents did. She considered it natural and sensible to believe because her parents' lives had shown that God was good, but she didn't have any feelings about it, and never expected to. Several others people in that particular congregation were extremely suspicious of anyone who said they 'felt' blessed, or happy or liberated. Such talk was labeled as being 'holier than thou'.

The time came when Mrs. Webster was no longer able to maintain and care for the home she had lived in since she married. She applied to enter a 10-storey building built by three local churches for people who were no longer able to manage the responsibilities of home ownership. She began to sell and give away all the accumulations of a lifetime of marriage and raising children. "I think I should tell you," she said to me one Sunday, after service, "I have a feeling, a strong feeling. I feel as if someone is with me all the time I am packing up my home and getting ready to move. I feel someone is always there, comforting me and telling me it will be alright where I am going."

God keeps faith, with people who believe because their parents did, and with people who continue in the faith and never feel a thing. God had come to her when she was at her loneliest and most distressed and given her the feelings she had had a right to all along. How gentle our God is. Later Mrs. Webster told me that she still felt the presence. She looked 10 years younger, a combination of the security of the new home and the presence that accompanied her.

Did Abraham always feel blessed? When people asked him how he was, did he reply that he was guarded and protected by the only God and that he was blessed and called to be a blessing? I think he did: he was a leader as well as a strong believer. The record says that, when he built his second altar, he called upon the Lord. One of the meanings of that word is to preach the Lord. Young choose this meaning when he

made his modern translation of the Bible.   So Abraham
probably felt blessed. As for Sarah, she probably felt weepy,
with good reason, and did not feel blessed. Her time would
come.

Chapter 11

LOOKING LIKE A LOOSER

If you go to the right, I will go to the left.

"You have a choice.' Those were magical words we heard when we were young. We could choose a career, a spouse, even the house where we lived with our spouses. Now the magic has quite gone – stolen by a generation of parents with child-managements skills, who have turned choice into law, like this: 'You have a choice eat your broccoli and get dessert, or leave your broccoli and get no dessert." The magic word 'choice' now fills me with gloom; dinner without dessert. What kind of a meal is that?

Abraham's nephew had a choice, and he was no longer a young man. He had been with Abraham ever since Abraham left Ur and stayed in Haran. Now Lot was rich, and his uncle was even richer. The men taking care of their herds of animals had begun to quarrel over available space to graze animals and pitch tents.

"You have a choice," said Abraham to Lot. But this was no child-management law; this was the word of opportunity. "We need to separate to prevent quarrelling between me and you, and between our herders." So it had got to that, had it? Lot had begun to quarrel with Abraham, and Abraham had begun to search for a peaceful solution. Was separation the only peace they could devise? Lot continued to need Abraham, and perhaps childless Abraham was going to miss his only male relative. I live in an era when angry congregations separate from their home congregations and go their own way. I wish it weren't so: both sides need each other in ways that will only become apparent long after the separation.

"You go in one direction and I'll go in the other," said Abraham to his nephew. Lot chose to go in the direction of the fertile valley, leaving for Abraham the tops and sides of the mountains.

When this story of Abraham and Lot is read in discussion groups, people are quick to denounce the selfishness of Lot, but too embarrassed to talk about Abraham because he looks like the looser. The more straightforward speakers in a group will even say that Abraham came out of the negotiation looking like a fool. This is useful of course, because it opens the door for questions and reflection. Was Abraham foolish, or too hasty with a half-thought-out solution? Did he care about Lot so much that he willingly gave him the best, or was his confidence in God's provision so great that it made him generous?

I sold real estate for two years after I retired from being a pastor. (I needed a change from too many funerals and too few baptisms.) Another retired minister joined the staff of the franchise where I worked. His name will have to be Herbert because I can't give you his real name, but this story is true. "Business and Christianity don't mix," he said. "Christianity is about getting right with God and going to heaven; business is about making as much money as you can for your client: you can't do both things at the same time." At the time I had no quick reply but it wouldn't have changed things anyway because Herbert didn't converse: he just pronounced. When I returned home and reported the conversation to David, he said, "Ask him if that applies to carpenters?"

Herbert had erected a wall between what he believed and what he did. It's an old heresy that says, my soul will go to heaven; therefore it belongs to God but my brain belongs to my body, and will die, and therefore I can do what I choose.

Most of what I did as a pastor was to help people break down that mental wall that separates religious thought from daily actions. Individuals become new people when they break down the partition they have made in their minds, and allow faith in God to infiltrate every daily choice until both soul and body is one great lake of unity with God.

Abraham knew what we forget: that we should demonstrate the goodness of God in every action we do. Whether it's eating and drinking, or whether it's avoiding conflict between family members, we should act so that God's goodness is demonstrated by our actions. (We call it "Doing all to the glory of God".) The Apostle Paul knew this and he wrote that he didn't think about what was best for himself but what was best for others. Paul urges us to follow his example.

O.K. so we did this! All through those long years of raising the children; consistently we did what was best for them, and put ourselves second to their welfare. Now they are grown up; isn't it time to please ourselves? How long do we go on doing this? The awful thing is there is no end to it, and it doesn't just apply to putting our children's good before our own, but to our neighbors, people at work and people in church. Even to the nephew who is quarreling with us. We are to consider their good and choose what is good for them rather than what is good for us. We do this so that through us they may learn about the goodness of God.

Now there is an escape route that Christians frequently use: the argument that what is best for everyone is a system of firm rules and strong consequences. We unblushingly say that we ourselves have been subject to firm rules and strong consequences. We even imply that this is why we are such righteous people. This way of escape says that doing good to our neighbor means setting rules and making consequences when our rules are not followed, even when the consequences are disastrous to their welfare.

Abraham didn't use the escape routes; he applied his own rules to his own behavior and didn't impose them on Lot, who certainly knew about them. The only consequence that Lot experienced was his own discovery that the best pasture land was not the best social environment. And even when he discovered that, Abraham was there to help him and never told him that he had made his bed and must lay on it.

We who are Christians have not been subjected to strong rules and consequences, but to repeated forgiveness and to the unfailing help of God our Father. Jesus came to save us while we were still defying God. God says that he has held out his hands all day to a nation that was ignoring him. What we have received is grace, the good that we don't deserve. If we are to follow the example of God, and His Son Jesus we are to offer grace and forgiveness, support and help to every other person.

Where do we find the strength to go on living in this sacrificial way? From God himself who, as is shown in the next part of Abraham's story, is not just watching how we choose but is standing ready to support and befriend us.

Chapter 12

EXPLORING THE FAITH
Walk through the land, the length and breadth of it.

Abraham had just given away half of his nomadic route. Now the best pasture land was no longer open to him and his herders. Perhaps he even looks a bit regretfully at the valley pastures. God gives him a command. "Rise," says God, "Walk through this land, walk the length of it, walk the breadth of it because I will give it to you." Reassured, Abraham returns to the Oaks of Mamre in Hebron and builds another altar.

It's a safe conclusion that when the priests were collating the various oral and written records of the scriptures they chose the parts which were valid and valuable. The fact that they left in this phrase, 'walk through the land' suggests that they believed it had a meaning for the people who were to follow.

Before our family went to live in Kansas City, Missouri, I bought a map. Kansas City is flat territory and so the grid system has no breaks and dead ends, the map is a pleasure of simplicity to look at. I drew a circle round the place where we were to live and memorized the names of the streets nearby. It was all book knowledge, but in the spirit of the song; "This Land Is Our Land" I felt like I owned Kansas City and I wasn't there yet.

In the wonderfully hot summer of 1973 I walked those streets, and we drove them, exploring the clean friendly city and all of its treasures. Faith is like this. There is a kind of faith that people own because they have learnt it from a book, or believed what they heard in church. They call it 'their faith' but they haven't really acted upon it, it is just a firm conviction and a beloved concept, a folded up map that they like to talk about.

Eventually faith gets challenged. We are faced with a choice or an opportunity to do something we have not done before. It could be an opportunity to do good to someone even at our own expense, or it could be a choice to tell the truth when a lie would be more convenient. Whenever we make the right choice it is a step of faith, we step out of the mental concepts into the streets of faith. It is surprising but there are a great many people in church who have not stepped off their map of religious dogma and out into the streets of the life of faith. They believe one thing and do another. When I question people about their reluctance to put shoes on their faith and walk around in the arena of faith, the reason they most often give is that the faith action involves a risk. Eventually, if they stay in the faith community and listen to the stories other people tell them, they get the courage to take the risk. The result is exhilarating. They decide to try another activity and suddenly they are walking the streets of faith. Faith increases with use, as they act according to the nature of faith their confidence in the goodness of God increases. They are alive to God, their life is no longer limited to the 'now' but assimilates the future. They no longer walk alone; they are accompanied.

When I read the words of God to Abraham, I understand

them as spoken to me also, "Get up, and walk through the land, the length of it and the breadth of it, for I will give it unto you." God wants to give us faith; he wants to increase our faith. He speaks to us, through scripture, telling us to take possession of the gift of faith and begin to explore it; experience its hills and valleys. As we do this a life stirs within us which we know is not the pale thing we called life before but is God living in us and through us, and we are told that the new life of God within us will continue past death, into futures we have not yet seen on any map.

Chapter 13

PRIESTLY GRANDPARENTS
King Melchizedek, priest of God Most High

There was frequent warfare among the small tribes and petty kings. One way of acquiring live-stock and slaves was to attack and raid the neighboring tribe. Abraham's nephew Lot was captured and carried away in one of those raids. Abraham went to rescue him. He defeated the raiders and returned with the people and property that he had rescued. He brought them back to their homes and kinsfolk, Rulers and citizens greeted their rescued relatives, and hoped for the return of their property. Into this scene walks a priest carrying bread and wine.

In the 12 months I spent being a chaplain intern in Methodist Medical Center St. Joseph, I was always a priest coming into the scene. There were many scenes. Once, in a moment of shock, a mother let her baby slide out of her arms. I was there to pick up the baby (she wasn't hurt) and hold it . I was there to stand beside that mother while she heard the news that one of her children was terribly injured. I stayed there, doing nothing, except holding the baby and being there. A year after, I met that mother again and she told me that it had been truly helpful to have a person who was obviously a friend materialize at that moment.

I was a priest who came into the hospital room when the lights were still on at 2 a.m. who listened to fears without saying that they were groundless. I was a priest when an angry visitor attacked the security guard and the guard sent for a Chaplain because he was too sorry for the distraught visitor to escort him out of the building. I was a priest who came out of the corridor into the room where a mother held her new-born baby for the only two hours it lived.

I was a priest not only because the New Testament says that all believers are priests but because the Church had piloted the Chaplaincy program and because that hospital authorized me to represent the whole Christian Church to everyone in the building.

There was a difference between being a pastor and a chaplain that I treasured. As a pastor, people came to me; as a chaplain, I went to them. The coming into their presence was, to me, always a sacred re-enactment of the Son of God coming into the world to seek and to save.

A priest doesn't just come personally into a scene; a priest is a representative of the Most High God, and of the Church. When the priest comes in so does the power of the Church that trained and approved and authorized that action. Within that authority are contained the prayers of the church that sponsors the mission. When a priest is present both the power of Christ and of His Church is present with his representative.

At Abraham's hour of triumph a priest was present. Unlike my hospital patients and staff, Abraham was not in need of comfort and friendship. He was a winner returning in victory, neither sad nor suffering. (Unless you can call having a nephew who didn't know how to choose the right place to live, suffering.) But it was appropriate that the priest should appear at Abraham's time of triumph because he was there to mediate God's blessing to Abraham and Abraham's praise to God. Abraham was already blessed and had the promise that he would be even more blessed, yet he accepts the priest's blessing. He recognized that to be involved with this representative of God was to be blessed. It's still the same; you can refuse the blessing, but you can't avoid the chance. It comes with the priest.

And whose priest is he? This land was already filling up with immigrant tribes, each praying to their own tribal god. Is he a priest of the sun, or the moon, or the stars? Does he represent the fertility god? No, he is the priest of the God who possesses Heaven and Earth. Interestingly enough, the people with many gods knew Melchizedek's God as 'The Tallest God'. That phrase gets translated into 'Most High God.'

So Abraham wasn't alone in his worship of the One God. There were others. The self-revelation of God had only just begun. They knew so little, but they knew that the One God was the great God. How did they learn it? By the telling of stories, the stories Seth told to Enos, and Enos told to Cainan, and Cainan told to Mahalalele, and Mahalaleel told to Jared, and Jarad told to Enoch, and Enoch told to Methuselah, and Methuselah told to Lamech, and Lamech told to Noah. And then the process began all over again because Noah told Shem, Ham, and Japheth. May I ask about you: to whom are you telling the story? It seems a priestly task for grandparents, especially because grandparents can add their own part of the sacred story to the great story.

The priest has three major tasks:

- □ to offer the sacrifice;
- □ to introduce God to man, and man to God;
- □ to keep the records of the sacred story.

God has made those who trust him into a nation of priests, and everyone who trusts Jesus has the privilege of carrying out those same priestly duties.

In the days when the Church called everyone a priest according to the New Testament but did not help women carry out all of the priestly tasks, I understood that I had inherited the New Testament priesthood of all believers; but I was compelled to recognize that no one was very interested in helping me immerse my life in that calling. So I initiated an agreement with God. I would be his minister and the world would be my parish. It sounds spiritual and enlightened, but it was lonely and I lacked sufficient training, not that I let that stop me. I lacked the support of other ministers. There was a lot of evidence that God accepted my ministry, but if the Church had authorized it sooner it would have been a much stronger ministry.

I still visualize Abraham's return with Lot: the noisy crowd, weeping their thanks and shouting their joy at seeing their sons and brothers return home, the rulers coming out to meet Abraham, and into it all walking the priest of the Most High God. I see Abraham receiving the bread and wine, and then Abraham, the members of his army, the priest, and perhaps all the others, praising God for the victory he had granted. What a privilege we all have, for we have all been made priests. But how greatly that privilege is enhanced when we have been authorized and trained to carry out a specific part of the priestly service, and we have not only sponsorship but a group we can report to. As a hospital chaplain intern, I reported daily in a written report but then I spent an hour each week with my mentor. His sole purpose was to help me refine the care which I gave to those who accepted my services. One afternoon each week all four chaplains met with our mentor and related one incident of caring that we wanted to examine in the presence of others. We wrote reports of the exact words we had said. The other chaplains suggested ways we could have refined the care we were giving.

Now that everyone in the Church understands that we are all ministers we get a very mixed bunch of ministers. Some ministry has been trained and reflected upon, some has been guided and some is just haphazard attempts undertaken by people who understand very little about what they are attempting. Sometimes we receive wise direction from the other priests we look to for support and sometimes we receive parroted words from the latest spiritual self-help book. You would think, wouldn't you, that such a privileged office as a priest of the Most High God deserves some preparation and training. Sadly, the people who have been elected to decision-making bodies are still preferring common sense above spiritual sense.

In my first solo pastorate, I suggested to the ruling body (called Session) that we spend some of the special offering taken for the purpose of evangelism. "Oh no", replied one of the elders, "I've never believed in spending money just because we have it." Solemnly the others agreed, "You never know when we might need that money." I asked whether the group thought that God was somehow poor and needed to economize on resources. The group looked at me and thought perhaps I was trying to make them look foolish.

I left that church and asked God to send me somewhere where the leaders of the church had spiritual vision and courage. It didn't happen. Instead, I spent the next two years as pulpit supply to churches with empty pulpits. What a lot I learnt. How valuable to me such a varied background became. But I never did find a group of leaders with vision and courage. There are such groups, but they have many applicants, people who have gone to famous seminaries and achieved numerical and financial success in previous churches. I didn't know it then, but I didn't stand a chance. God did know it but he evidently didn't think it important.

Chapter 14

WHAT EARTHLY USE IS THAT TO ME?

I have given this land to your descendants

What on earth is the good of that to me? No, Abraham never said that, but did you? As you read about God's promise to Abraham that he would be the father of nations and kings, did you wonder what use that promise was to Abraham? He didn't even live long enough to see the birth of his twelve great grandsons. What use is a promise about something that will happen on this earth if you are dead and gone before it happens?

If it had been you to whom the promise was made, would you have wondered what earthly use was a promise of a future you would not see? The question is important because in a way it is to you that the promise is made. Spiritually or physically, you are part of the story and some of the innumerable descendants of Abraham are coming through you. Would you have been grateful for a promise that something wonderful would happen after you were dead? Was I? No, I wasn't. I rushed past the promise and concentrated on grasping every opportunity to do good or receive good while I lived. Just live the religious life to the full was my thinking.

I guess King Hezekiah was one person who wondered what the use of God's promise to Abraham was. King Hezekiah made a very good job of leading his nation. He sponsored the temple worship and had the book of Deuteronomy read publicly to the assembled people. During his life time a prophet told him that after he died the nation he had ruled would be defeated in battle, his descendants would be taken captive and terrible things would happen to them. His only response was that at least there would be peace in his life-time.

There is a tendency to concentrate so strongly on the heavenly aspect of our relationship with God that we loose the earthly. All who believe God's Word have a future in heaven, but what about this earth, and the people who are going to come after we have left? Because we will never see them, are we to live as though the earth ends when we die? Perhaps it's a pity that we ignore the earthly because of the spiritual. Maybe there is a great joy in knowing that the goodness of God will reach our descendents long after we are gone. One of the sorrows of being old is that we no longer have a future; we only have a past. We have lost our strength and our talents have become redundant. We have no resources to invest in a new future. We are stationary in time, waiting, just waiting, for the next life. Perhaps this is the time to nourish a future we shall never see, to find ways to influence the next generation.

In the days when the biblical events were happening the Assyrians defeated Israel, the Babylonians defeated the Assyrians, the Medes and Persians defeated the Babylonians, the Greeks defeated the Persians and the Romans defeated the Greeks. Great nations rise and fall like the waves of the ocean. Belonging to the greatest nation on earth might merely mean belonging to the next nation to topple. All of these nations left us something: their history, their museums and their influence. That influence has shaped Europeans and Americans today so that we are gifted by the lives of people who never knew us. In the same way our lives and what we do with the little time remaining to us will gift those who come after us.

It is true that Abraham did not see his twelve great grand-children. But he saw something else. Jesus said, "Your Father Abraham saw my day and rejoiced." Perhaps one answer to the puzzle is that we should make less of a hard line between our spiritual future and the earthly future; maybe we should blur the division a little. Blessings flow from God into this earth and into this time, and we are part of the now but also part of the future. Maybe an understanding of the presence of eternity within the now-ness of our lives will give meaning to the waiting, waiting, for the signal to come home.

Chapter 15

SARAH'S SORROW
Sarah gave Hagar to Abraham as a wife

When people remember the story of Sarah they never remember any bitterness. If Sarah was never bitter, she was far more virtuous than most of the women married to 'men-who-obey-God' today.

She had so much to be bitter about. Abraham sold her twice to save his life from foreign kings, but risked his life to save his nephew. Abraham gave the choice of pasture land to his nephew who chose the most fertile land, resulting in Sarah's husband not being as rich as he might have been if he had kept the best routes for himself. Most of all, where was Sarah when her husband and son set out carrying wood for a sacrifice without an animal to offer? Was this act so secret that she didn't know? Although they returned praising God for his great intervention, what were her feelings when she learned? What does it cost a woman to be married to a 'man-who-obeys God'?

When people in the church preach about the quarrel between Hagar and Sarah they are usually most careful to point out that having a child by another woman with your wife's consent was both moral and legal at that time. What they never stop to ask is, what did it cost Sarah to consent to another woman being in her husband's bed? When Sarah complained to her husband that it was 'all his fault,' why are there no recorded words of encouragement and understanding? At a time when a woman's chief value was her ability to bear children, it became obvious to all the herders and staff that Sarah was the infertile partner in the marriage. For all these things Sarai deserved at least the grateful thanks of her servant and husband. Instead, the servant despised her, and her husband chose not to get involved.

The servant girl did not have the sense to remain outwardly humble and grateful. Instead she despised Sarai, who in turn despised her. Sarah treated this poor pregnant girl so harshly that she ran away. The self-righteous amongst us (and I must admit there are a lot of us in church, because we concentrate more on how good we should be than on how good God is) would find it hard to have sympathy for the servant, but God does not find it hard. The angel of the Lord came searching for the scornful servant and gave to her the promise similar to the one he gave Abraham: 'I will greatly multiply thy descendants so that the multitude of them cannot be numbered. The servant obeyed the instruction to return home and submit to her mistress and came back to Abraham the father of her child, and Sarah who had mistreated her.

After the maid's return, how did Sarah feel? She lived childless in the same household as Abraham and Hagar who had both received the promise of a multitude of descendants. Did she ever feel over-looked by God? Did she ever despise herself for her inadequacy? Did she weep at night because of the seeming injustice of her situation? Other people besides Sarah have felt this way. They struggle against misfortune, struggle with personal inadequacies, and feel that there is no justice in life. Sarah's story has a happy ending; but Sarah had a long wait before her prayers were answered. The waiting time is long and hard for today's multitude of discouraged, disheartened people. Believing against evidence to the contrary is not easy.

For Hagar, the woman who was so badly treated that she ran away even whilst she was pregnant, there was an angel. The angel 'found' her and asked her questions, then gave her a promise. For both the Sarahs and the Hagars of today there is an angel who seeks the people that other people have forgotten about. That angel is the Spirit of God's presence among humans. That Spirit brings instructions and promises. God's Spirit supports those who have no other support, and those who have much support. It is all the same to God because we all shall be blessed and richly blessed, and we all shall be made a blessing.

Chapter 16

RE-INVENTING YOURSELF AT NINETY-NINE

His son and all his slaves were circumcised

W ell no, Abraham didn't re-invent himself. God did. He gave Abraham a new name, and turned Abraham's household into a nation.

How about us today? Can we be re-invented in our old age? God took something that Abraham had been doing for years and changed it into something greater. Like this: Abraham had been leading his household in worship ever since he built his first altar in Canaan. In Abraham's old age, God turned that household into a nation. They were not blood relatives of Abraham but they all accepted the sign of the covenant between God and them. Like Abraham they were gentiles but by entering into the covenant agreement with God, and accepting the sign of that covenant, which was circumcision they became the first part of the covenant nation. Years later when Joshua invaded Canaan, little groups of people called "the mixed multitude" already knew the God of Abraham and eagerly joined Joshua in his conquest.

Ishmael, Abraham's first-born child, son of Hagar, was thirteen years old when he was given the mark of the covenant; his Father was ninety-nine. Ishmael did not become a Jew but God honored the covenant that had been made with him and made him into a great nation.

My branch of the church baptizes infants when they are babies. People ask if it is right to give a religion to a child who cannot decide for himself. What we are doing is bringing the child into the covenant community which is the church. The parent/s and church members promise to raise the child in the faith, and without this we do not baptize. When the child reaches the age where he/she wishes to decide for himself the child confirms his/her baptism by affirming that Jesus is their Lord and Savior and that with God's help they renounce evil and will follow Jesus.

Some of these children forget the affirmation of their vows. I was amused one day when I was in the emergency room of a hospital to hear the admitting nurse ask a young man, probably in his twenties, what his religion was. (Hospitals used to do this so they could allow the clergy access to anyone who needed prayer.) The young man yelled through to the waiting room, "Mom what religion am I?"

'Baptist,' came the reply.

The young man told the nurse, "I'm, err, Baptist religion." When our four sons were born, we still belonged to the Assemblies of God church and they were all dedicated to God. We promised to consider them God's children and raise them on his behalf. I have never found anything to hesitate about between infant baptism and infant dedication. They are both covenants with God.

In the days when we kept the door of the church sanctuary open to the street so that anyone who wanted to could enter and pray, I was surprised by a young woman bursting into my office. "I am a baptised child of the Presbyterian Church," she told me with desperation in her voice, "and I want to return to my church and my parents." She had been, she told me, a long way away from both church and parents for most of her youth and into her twenties. Now she claimed her baptism. We church ministers got together to help. We found where her parents now lived (Presbyterians keep registers) and someone drove her to them. The most important thing to remember about a baptism or a dedication is that God keeps his end of the covenant. There is comfort in knowing that fact during the years when the baptized child is wandering far from home and church.

Abraham was ninety-nine when God reinvented him into the leader of a great nation. I haven't met many people who have been reinvented in their old age but I have met a few. There are the old people who marry for a second or third time in their old age and start out all over again with adjustments and changes. There are those wonderful relatives, usually women, who leave their own home to go and live with a relative who is dying, reinventing themselves from the comfort of a retired leisurely life to one of cooking, cleaning and nursing. Most wonderful of all are the grandmas who bring the grandchildren into their own home because their mother is alone and too sick to care for them. I admit I have no desire to be reinvented. I have just acclimatized myself to the freedom of retirement and I would hate to give it up now. I remember that God is a surprising God, and that frightens me a little.

Abraham's reinvention included a new name. His name up till then had been Abram. God changed it to Abraham. Abraham meant 'Father of a multitude'. At the time, he was the father of one child. If he'd given himself that name, we'd say that he was exercising great faith. However it wasn't Abraham but God who chose that name, God was demonstrating his own confidence in his own word.

Most of us gained a new name when we began to be called Grandad and Grandma. David and I refused those names. They made us feel old. It is only now when I've had the name for over a quarter of a century that I begin to see possibilities. I didn't see them by myself either. It was my grown children who helped me to see that being a grandparent could be a calling.

God gave Sarah a new name too. She had been Sarai, now she became Sarah. Looking the new name up in Strong's Hebrew dictionary, I had the good fortune to notice 'Sar' before I turned to 'Sarah'. As many of you know, 'ah' is the suffix which indicates a female noun. Sarah is the feminine of Sar and Sar is shown by James Strong as meaning a head person, captain, general, governor, keeper, lord, master or prince. The popular explanation of Sarah's name is princess, but her name can also mean woman-captain, woman-general, woman-governor. I prefer these meanings because it shows that God's estimation of Sarah was not that of a princess, who is often powerless over her own life, but that of someone who could lead and make decisions.

In between instructing Abraham about these two great make-overs, God reminds him that he is going to have a son by Sarah-The-Elderly [only God doesn't call her that]. Abraham, the newly named Father of a Multitude laughs, "It's already too late," he reminds God. "She's long past the age at which women can become pregnant." Resignation and hopelessness produce hollow laughter. God goes on to tell him that great things will happen to Ishmael also, and Abraham apparently forgets to tell Sarah about the promised child.

Cora, a member of the first church I was pastor of, questioned one of my sermons. "You say that we all have gifts and talents," she said. "I have none. I've been a widow for years so I'm not a home-maker, my only child lives far away so I'm not a parent, and the only skill I learnt when I was working was a skill that is redundant now."

That was Cora's opinion of herself. I visited her when she was in hospital and prayed for her. After I had finished, Cora took my hand in both of hers and began to pray out loud. She thanked God for my helpful sermons, for my love for the congregation, for my hard work and imagination with the children. Now tell me she had no gifts! In that first church, no one loved me very much. I was a woman minister in the days when people thought the Bible said women should keep silent [the other women were not very silent on that topic]. I had followed a dearly loved man who had been there 25 years and I was not doing anything as well as he had. "Cora, your prayers are your gift," I said. "Furthermore, your appreciation of me has strengthened me."

Perhaps Cora's gift was more valuable than all the other gifts in that church. Her continued appreciation and encouragement strengthened me to continue serving all the people in the building. The day I left she stood at the head of the church steps and wept. The memory of those tears reassured me in the following days when I thought I had failed at the work of being a pastor.

Genuine appreciation, encouragement and thoughtful prayers: I do believe they are the greatest gifts anyone can give and although we have less energy and our memories become a little slow, these gifts are still available for us to practice and distribute to those around us.

Chapter 17

LAUGHTER AND LIES
Why did Sarah laugh?

It was Abraham who named Isaac, but God who chose the name. The name means laughter. Does God laugh? We laugh and we are made in the likeness of God. So yes, I think God laughs. I think he enjoyed the joke when he told this unbelieving pair of elderly people that they would have a son in their very old age.

God talks to Abraham again, to tell him once more that Sarah will have a son. Abraham does not laugh this time. He had protested the unlikeliness of this before and been silenced. I do think that God laughed with Sarah and Abraham when they laughed and laughed at the joy of holding Sarah's own baby son. God's purpose and desire for humanity is to bless them, to make them happy, and on this occasion when his purpose was so clearly achieved I like to think that he laughed. The New Testament says that the Master of the faithful servants says to them, "Enter into the joy of your Lord." Joy will surely involve laughter. Abraham and Sarah had laughed before: laughs of bitter resignation and hopelessness. God had not been angry with either of them.

Sarah had laughed silently within herself, but God had heard the laughter. Reassuring isn't it, that when we laugh in bitter resignation or laugh at the impossibility of something, God hears. This time God asks a question, "Why did Sarah laugh?" Following the custom of the time, she was not included in the conversation, but God asked where she was and included her. Being included is a way of being loved, respected and recognized; it is life changing. The churches of our time are learning this lesson, and everywhere we look we see the church experiencing the powerful results that come from including people who have been excluded. The church has learnt how to listen to people who have never been listened to before, the despised, the hated, the abused. We are teaching those people how to give voice to their pains so that everyone will hear. The results are miraculous, but since the modern age distrusts miracles we call it affirmation. A little while ago, a group of Presbyterians visited a group of our national enemies and asked them why they are so angry with us. Many people in the church were shocked: we were honoring the dishonorable, but many other people thought we were loving our enemies.

The customs of the time did not honor women, but God does not follow local customs. He asks where Sarah is and then talks directly to her. Perhaps it was because the laughter was inward that Sarah thought she could deceive herself and her maker, and say that she did not laugh. Sarah lied to God. The Bible does not leave us wondering why, but tells us clearly that she was afraid. It is a terrible thing to lie to the creator because it involves lying to ourselves first, and if we lie to ourselves then we do not have the ability within ourselves to know our own truth because we are so busy hiding part of it. Sarah was a believer. She had acknowledged without anger that God had withheld the joy of having babies from her. What would happen now that she had both laughed and lied in the presence of God? "Yes, you did laugh," was his response, and that was all: no anger, no vengeance. What we know now is that whether we laugh within ourselves or cry within ourselves, God hears.

God understands that we are humans, with finite minds and limited understanding of what is involved in our partnership with him. He is gentle and patient, but that doesn't mean he accepts our unbelief. Instead he helps us believe. For Sarah, the help began immediately and she never had occasion to doubt again.

Earth rings with laughter. Peals of joy, relief and amazement ring through the universe and reach the ears of angels. People who had thought that they would always be sad find comfort and begin to laugh again. People who have been despised laugh when they are respected. People whose development has been arrested, laugh with amazement when they discover the changes that are happening within themselves. I remember asking a student if there had been any difference in his life since he asked God to be his God. He said, "All my life I was angry at many things. I always had a chip on my shoulder. I left the church that day and as I started to walk towards the dormitory I realized something was missing. I didn't have a chip on my shoulder, so I turned round to look for it and was so surprised that I shouted out loud, "Look at that! It's gone!'"

Changed people laugh with amazement. Frightened people laugh with relief. Lonely people laugh with their families. God hears and rejoices. His good purposes are bursting through the gray mists of earth and drawing us into his eternal joy.

Chapter 18

GOD'S SMALL REQUIREMENT
That he may train his children to keep God's ways

It should have been a wonderful evening. But before Abraham and Sarah had time to share their excitement about the promised child God decides to involve Abraham in matters of state. He takes Abraham into his confidence and tells him that he intends to examine the citizens of Sodom and Gomorrah because a great cry of outrage has gone up to God. God wants to know how great is the sin of these cities before he takes measures to restrain the evil that is practiced there.

God was not willing, the prayer book tells me, to be God without us. He did not need us because he does not have needs, but he chose us. He chose to make us partners in his activities. Now God confides in Abraham, "because," says God, "I know him: that he will follow the way of Jehovah and train his family and household to do righteousness and justice even after he has passed on."

What a little thing! Training his family and the people he employed to walk in God's path, to do right and be just. Because of this God treats Abraham as a friend and partner.

Isn't this the sort of thing that every good parent tries to do? It seems a bit basic and we would have expected God to be using a different assessment. Moses, Daniel and David were men of courage who led a nation and confronted emperors. In contrast, all God looks for in Abraham is the ability to train a family in the ways of Jehovah.

Sometimes, but not often, I worked with men and women who were uncomfortable with my calling to be a preacher. They told me that all God required of me was to raise my children well. Maybe they were right. At the time, all I could see was that if one generation devoted themselves to raising the next generation who in turn would devote themselves to raising another generation? How would we ever reach the people who did not know God? Something within me drove me, compelled me, to be ever trying to reach God's absentee children and bring them back to be at home with God. Now I look back, and like all parents I wonder if I did the right thing. I ask would the children have had a better chance if I had devoted myself exclusively to their welfare? But all four of our children are happy and successful so I feel reassured.

Even the male members of God's family of faith might have a problem with the simplicity of God's requirement: a life centered on God, and revolving around training family and household to walk in the path of Jehovah. I can imagine the men asking if God wouldn't prefer them to lead a nation, establish a new denomination or at least discover some startling new truth in the Bible.

There is a curious statement in the book of Hebrews. The writer says that in a way the Levite great great grandsons of Abraham were included in Abraham's action when he gave a tenth of his gains to a priest called Melchizedek. The writer is interested in proving that there can be other priests besides the sons of Levy. I used to concentrate on finding who Melchizedek was and overlooked the strange statement that if

Abraham did it, then in a way his descendents did it! Now I'm fascinated with that casual statement. Have we in some way unknown to us passed onto our children through many generations our patterns and values?

Our generation has recognized that we are in some way inheritors of the mistreatment of the native American nations and the enslaving of the African nations, and that we bear some limited responsibility to try to correct what our ancestors did. Is this an example of the unborn generation being involved in the actions of the ancestor? If that is so, when we choose to do right and be just and walk in the way of The Almighty, do our descendents inherit what we have chosen? It seems more likely than unlikely. Will a godly lifestyle pass on to future generations something that will be healthy and satisfactory and form a platform for developing the likeness of God in humanity? If that is so, and since God is faithful, it seems likely, that our living has already born fruit.

I like to form theories about why God waited so long to give faithful, long-suffering Sarah her own baby. Of course this proved that the birth was miraculous and the baby was a special gift of God. But did God have another reason for waiting? Was it only when Abraham and Sarah became old that they had the experience and self-discipline to inculcate in Isaac a life-style acceptable to God? We, who have become old, have experiences and learning to pass on to our grandchildren.

But even though the aged have gifts to give to their descendants, how do we give them? Since the Sixties, young people have not learnt from their parents, but from their peers. We, their parents, grieve because our experience and warnings are disregarded. Our only hope is that God will bless us by calling our children and grandchildren to himself in such a way that they will be able to stop resisting. In spite of the indifference of a younger generation and in spite of the barriers to sharing our experience of God ['Don't force them, don't embarrass them, you'll drive them away' etc.] God may choose to bless our remembered lives by revealing himself to our grandchildren. Perhaps this is likely since God says that because Abraham follows the way of Jehovah and trains his family group to do so, he can fulfill his promises to Abraham.

So, from the life of Abraham we have gathered at least three principles for the work of growing old with God. First: God has called us his friends and wants to involve us in his activities. Second: intercessory prayer respect and affirmation are perhaps the most valuable gifts we can give to God by giving them to others. Third: what God requires of us is to train our families to do justice, love kindness and walk humbly with God.

Chapter 19

PRAYING FOR THE UNDESERVING

Will you sweep away the righteous also?

God had not said he would destroy Sodom and Gomorrah; he had only said he would visit them and know. Abraham interpreted that to mean that he would destroy the city. Why did he think that? Because Abraham knew what continual and destructive evil was being practiced in those cities. But now God was visiting those cities to 'know' what they were doing. It was C.S Lewis who first made me aware that, although it is important for people to know God, it is much more important to be known by God. What God would know about the two cities would cause him to end the cruelty and corruption that was breeding there. What God knows about those who have trusted him and obeyed him is that they are his.

Abraham begins to negotiate with God. Earlier Abraham had prayed for Ishmael and God had accepted and granted that prayer. (Are today's Christians praying for the descendents of Ishmael or are we just hoping for their defeat?) Now

Abraham begins to intercede for the wicked cities. God actually encourages him by agreeing to every request Abraham makes. This encouragement signifies that God is willing to be entreated on behalf of others. We call it intercessory prayer; it is what Jesus did and is doing for us. Abraham's prayer for Ishmael was the first recorded prayer of intercession.

I want to ask you why Abraham didn't want the city destroyed. Our practice has been to remove anything that could spoil or destroy. We kill rats, remove rotten fruit from baskets of good food, we lock away the people who may hurt society, and kill our enemies. Why didn't Abraham think the world would be better off without the citizens of Sodom and Gomorrah who had broken the honored code of protection of guests and hospitality to travelers, intended to mob rape and were determined to kill Lot when he tried to oppose them? I ask you, what was Abraham thinking of? Didn't he want to purge out the evil in order to preserve society?

Did Abraham have the notion that if there were fifty righteous people in those two cities then the presence and lives of those people would rescue the city from the evil of the rest of their society? It's preposterous, but I think it is true. It only took one prophet to convince Nineveh to change. Daniel's one action convinced King Nebuchadnezzar that God is truly the greatest of gods, the Lord-Over-Kings. Daniel's three friends convinced the king that their God should be honored throughout the nation. Jesus said that his followers were the salt of the earth, meaning people who stop the spread of decay.

If this is true, then our goal should not be to destroy the people who threaten society but to work together with God for their transformation.

Abraham is called 'The friend of God'. I think it is because his prayer coincided with the great purpose of God. God is not willing that anyone should perish, but he is willing that everyone should come to him to receive light and transformation.

Our grandchildren echo this prayer. "God bless Granddad and Grandma," they lisp as they say their prayers before they go to sleep. God hears the prayers of children, and grants them. That's one reason why you and I are so blessed today.

I look back and wonder what I did to deserve all the happiness I have had, and then I remember that I didn't deserve it. God granted it to me because other people prayed for me. There was an army of relatives, pastors and teachers daily praying for God's blessing on my life. How well their prayers have been answered.

What a great work this is, to pray for other people and to unite with God in his intentions and purposes, to ask for the gift he wants to give, to call down his blessings on other people. The wonderful thing about prayer is that long after we have left this life, God will still be answering those prayers. The work of changing society through prayer has been entrusted to the friends of God. Particularly it is available to older people because they have time to pray. The ability to pray is not hindered by lack of energy, inability to drive, or shortage of funds. Intercessory prayer, the greatest work of all, is wide open to all who wish to participate in it.

Having said that, I must admit that it is not easy to begin a life-style of prayer. I have friends who follow this life-style. Recently, when I had a health emergency, these friends phoned me regularly and prayed for me over the phone. I can understand that making a practice of praying with the sick over the telephone might sometimes be refused or resented, particularly if a person has just sat down to supper. They persevered; they almost forced their prayers on me. My health recovered, I walked out of the doctor's office with a smile so great that it stretched my face, I couldn't resist it, I annouunced to all the bored faces in the waiting room: "I don't have cancer." Only one of the bored faces smiled, the rest just waited for their turn. A life-style of prayer calls for something called discipline. Discipline, you remember, is the spiritual word for exercise. Like following a physical system of daily exercising, it needs special allotments of time, a program that builds slowly from smaller to greater lengths of time, and some initiative and excitement in choosing which nations to pray for and which national leaders to adopt as petition personnel. Then it is part of the spiritual exercise, to choose an enemy or enemies to pray for. 'Bless those who treat you badly', said Jesus.

In my Assembly of God days I found it easier to pray with a group in a prayer meeting. When I joined the Presbyterian church I never found a lot of help in group prayers. I remember standing in the twilight in a public place holding up candles and praying in silence. That way didn't work for me. I wanted to be back in a room where people prayed out loud, spontaneously and passionately, somewhere where I could say loud "Amen's" to someone else's prayers, and be stimulated to form my own requests. But I have discovered prayer books: the original Church of England Book of Common Prayer, the Presbyterian Book of Common Worship and a borrowed one from the Methodists. I get an enormous amount of spiritual reinforcement from the comprehensive form of these stylized prayers, feeling the force of praying with thousands of people who lived before me and prayed these same prayers.

In the same way that physical exercise benefits from having a trainer and a support group, so prayer benefits from having a leader and a group Often this is not available and a person must make their own schedule and find their own practices. I am convinced that nothing we can do for a person is as valuable as asking God to bless them.

One of the pastors in our presbytery once amused me by telling me the many ways he was able to augment his legal salary whilst managing a Nine-Eleven store. Listening to him, I thought that it must have taken an unusual miracle to change him from a man without much of a conscience into a dedicated pastor. I asked him how he came into an obedient relationship with God, and I expected a dramatic story. But he simply answered, "A praying mother. One day I acknowledged that what I was doing was wrong, and asked God to change me." So simple. So sublime.

Chapter 20

WHY DON'T THEY GROW UP TO BE LIKE US?

God remembered Abraham and sent Lot away

Did God love Abraham more than he loved Lot? Do grandparents love one child more than another? Should they? If you extend the family circle wide enough you will usually find a difficult family member, someone who doesn't make good choices and can't develop healthy habits. Abraham didn't have to extend his circle very far. He had a nephew, called Lot, who kept on making the wrong choices and needing help. Did Abraham become intolerant of Lot?

In the past, strict parents drove the pregnant unmarried daughter out of the house, rather than share her shame [and the expense?]. Today, the young, pregnant unmarried daughter often runs away from loving parents. Sometimes, the parents want to raise their grandchildren themselves, and some daughters run and hide rather than let that happen. Then there are the young sons who drive too fast, don't pay their traffic tickets, drive without licenses, don't make car payments and borrow their parents car to drive out of state. After a long time, the son returns home but the car never does.

"What would God do?" I ask the vexed relatives of difficult people.

"But I'm not God," they reply.

"No, you're not," I reply, "but if you're looking for an example of good parenting he's the best model to pattern your actions on."

I've known a great many difficult family members. Caring for them as a pastor was not hard. Often, difficult relatives are charming, interesting and flattering towards everybody but their own family. It was easy for my congregation to pray for these difficult people, to write to them and want news of them. But usually it was not the church who paid the child support and court costs. Abraham was the one who had to pay the costs. He had to bring his domestic army and engage in a dangerous battle on behalf of Lot who would not have been captured if he hadn't been living in the wrong place to begin with.

Lot wasn't a bad person. We can only guess why he liked living in a place that tormented his righteous soul by lawless conduct. Was he weary of sheep and shepherding? Did he want to be a part of the progress that was happening in those cities beside the Dead Sea of salt? We don't know. What we do know is that he wasn't bad but just made bad choices. Three times the apostle Peter calls him 'righteous Lot' and contrasts him with the people he was living amongst. Jesus talked about the days when Lot was alive and compared them to the last days.

Lot's willingness to appease a crowd of angry men by offering to allow them to have sexual relationships with his two engaged but unmarried daughters was evil, even though the code of honor at that time was to protect your guests with your very life. We rise up in angry condemnation, and so we should. We consider ourselves moral, but are there evils that we subscribe to because they are accepted and widely practiced, or because we consider them necessary to ensure our safety?

"What makes him/her act that way?" say puzzled grandparents? They ask, because they believe that if they could only find out what went wrong they could put it right. They so much want the difficult relative to change and become a relative they can be pleased with.

Lot didn't change. Consider the chances he had, the experiences which should have turned him around: he was taken captive but his uncle rescued him; the town where he lived was utterly destroyed but angels came and warned him to leave town. Still Lot didn't change. The angels told him to run to the hills for safety, but Lot said he'd like to live in a town. He chose a little town and something there made him so afraid that he took his two daughters and went to live in a cave. Sometimes, grandparents have to accept that the difficult family members are not going to change a whole lot. Once that fact is accepted, it's easier to love the difficult person just as they are without trying to fix them or force them to change. I used to advise grandparents to accept that some people can't please their relatives. "In that case," I'd say, "follow God's example and love them as they are."

How did God love Lot? Let me tell you about God's love for Lot. When he went to live in a cave, his daughter's chances of marriage became nil. Family was important in the days of tribal marriages. Lot's daughters realized they had no chance of marrying so they got their father drunk, and when he was drunk they went into his bed and had children by him. This disgusts us so much that our tendency is to think that this is the end! We imagine that from this day forward neither God nor Abraham will have anything to do with Lot or his daughters and certainly not with Moab or Ammon, the children born of incest. Yet Moses tells us that when he led the escapees from Egypt towards the home of their ancestors, that God warned him not to trouble the Moabites nor harrass the Ammonites because the land where those two tribes were living was land that God had given to them. "I have given that land as a possession to the descendants of Lot," was the message Moses heard from God. Before Israel entered into their land of promise, Lot's descendants were already living in their given land. They had done battle with some tall and strong inhabitants before they took that land.

Seemingly ungrateful and foolish relatives are loved by God. God gives inheritance to their children as well as to the children of Abraham. Because of your love and care and prayers, the difficult relatives are remembered in times of danger and their children are provided for and protected by God.

What remains now is to heal the sadness of grandparents who love the grandchildren and nieces and nephews and cousins and second cousins who didn't grow up into the kind of adults that they hoped for, to comfort them by reminding them that God remembers and will remember their labor of love, to encourage them to follow God's example and remind them that God helps those who try to imitate the way he loves.

Chapter 21

LAUGHING WITH SARAH
Everyone who hears me will laugh with me

In England, when you are looking for a new opportunity to be a pastor, people question you about your experience. In America, they question you about your qualifications. David and I, at ages forty-two and forty, had an abundance of experience; there seemed to be nothing in the church that we hadn't done. Qualifications were something different. We had no college education, and in the States it seems you can scarcely get through the door of the church office without a college degree. When our church was no longer able to financially support missionaries in Japan, we returned to England and cared for one of the Assembly of God's smallest and oldest churches. David, who owned his own business, worked five days a week and cared for the church on evenings and weekends. When he ran out of physical energy we decided to emigrate to Australia where David had a brother. (Actually he had a brother in New Zealand and a sister in Canada as well, so we had a good choice.) We were accepted for emigration and all that remained was to decide which city to go to. We spread a map of Australia on the floor of our living room along with a directory of Assembly of God churches and another directory of hospitals. [I had worked as a State Registered Nurse as well as a pastor's wife.]

The next day, we visited a church in the town where we were staying. At that time in English Assembly of God churches, people spoke in tongues spontaneously during the Sunday morning worship service and if someone received the interpretation, they spoke this out publicly. I think this practice has been discouraged since, because what was a reverent and disciplined way of responding to the Spirit of God became overwhelmed with hysteria and exhibitionism. The person who had received the interpretation stood up and said, "I have seen you with your maps spread out and your fingers pointing. Now put away your maps and be led by me." No one knew us at that church, we had spoken to no one and it was quite true that we hadn't asked the Lord's guidance: we had simply been led by our own good sense. So that was how we came to the United States, the last place we ever expected to be. There was a forgotten promise in our lives: when Philip our second son told his high school guidance counselor that he was going to go to college in the States I had responded, "Then I'll follow you there." Later it seemed impossible, and we decided we would ask Philip to come to Australia instead.

David and I were Americans in spirit and fitted in wonderfully. We loved most things about the states. Some things we hoped would change and by now most of them have, but we didn't have qualifications. All our lives David and I had read avidly and had entered several home-study programs with English colleges, but we longed for tutors. One day a college recruiter rang our home and asked if I would like to go to college. I replied, "Yes", but I had no money for fees.

He asked, "Can you get one hundred dollars?"

Carefully I replied, "I believe I can," and I don't think he understood that I was talking about believing in God, not in deposit accounts.

I went to college first. David went to Canada to open a new Teen Challenge Center. A year later I called him. I had graduated with honors. There is something called College Level Equivalency Program, and there was a way of giving credit for life experience, and I received credit for my nursing diploma. I was through college in a year. Someone quipped at the graduation ceremony that I should have received a certificate of non-attendance.

I called David in Canada. The new Teen Challenge Center was faltering badly. There had been a culture clash between American staff and Canadian values. I told him, "Park College gave me a financial scholarship. I asked them if I could give it to you instead: your first semester of college tuition is paid for."

Those were happy years: David's time at Park College and his following three years at St.Paul's Methodist Seminary. We laughed more in those years than all the years before. Sarah, are you listening?

Becoming a minister in the Presbyterian Church is like jumping through a series of hoops and climbing over a series of hurdles. It was harder for us because we didn't go to Presbyterian Seminaries. We tried to, but found no way of earning our support in strange states. Because I had started earlier, I was the first to become ordainable. Already working as a student supply, I was sitting in the church office, choosing speakers and hymns for my ordination service. Because I had been given a large number of papers containing other people's choices for ordination services I spread them on the floor and started to study them, sitting on the floor pointing here and there with my finger.

David called to ask if everything was going well. I replied, "It's finally going to happen." Both David and I are serious people. David even refused to smile for photographs, preferring instead to look thoughtful. I had been told in Seminary that I needed to smile more but I didn't see the need for it; it's the attitude that matters not the face. Suddenly, I was laughing outloud, peal after peal of laughter, crying huge sobs of relief and thankfulness at the same time. I carried on laughing and crying for a long time. I didn't try to regain control. It felt too good. Sarah had said that everyone who heard her laughing would laugh with her. I didn't know how literal the fulfillment of those words would be.

Like Abraham and Sarah, I also thought it was too late to receive something I had desperately hoped for. It wasn't a baby; we'd had four of them. It was a house: a nice, comfortable, labor-saving, pretty home. Why did I want pretty things? I am a pastor and vanity is not suitable to the life of a pastor. But I couldn't help it. I longed for comfort, convenience and prettiness. Our house in England, the one that was our dream house, was let out through an agency. After twelve years, the agency wrote and suggested we sell it. We did and what we did with the proceeds was pay off our debts. Two of us going through college and seminary had used up all the proceeds of that little dream house. I cannot describe how disappointed I was. Through another twelve years I watched the price of houses increase, until they were far beyond the possibility of our ever being able to buy again.

I really disliked living in church-owned houses. They were called manses and considered to be rent-free, but because we didn't pay rent that amount of money was deducted from the salary paid to us. That meant that when we retired we would not have a paid-up mortgage but would have to go on paying rent out of our pensions. 'Do you know," said one of the church members, "people are actually paying a hundred thousand dollars to buy a house! Who could afford to pay that much?"

As we drove past the new houses I sadly reminded myself that we were too old now to save that much and would never own our own home again. Still I couldn't help looking, and one day I took David to see the nicest condominium I had ever seen: brand new, with huge windows and surrounded by pretty landscaping. It was priced at one hundred thousand dollars. David and I had most of our lives served small congregations on small salaries, but in recent years David had been serving a seven-hundred member church. That congregation enjoyed doing good things for their three pastors. They had paid part of David's salary into a tax-exempt savings account ready for when he retired, and he had reached the age when he could draw it out without paying tax. The amount they had deposited came to exactly the amount needed for the down payment: ten thousand dollars. My two aunts had died leaving me one thousand dollars between them, just enough to pay closing costs and pay for the built-in appliances.

Our eldest son, Paul, who was single at the time, sent us a monthly amount which we used to make extra payments. With the help of Paul's money, the 25 year mortgage was paid off in eleven years, reminding me forever that in this present life, with God's help, it is never too late.

Chapter 22
PROMISES, PROMISES
Indeed I will bless you

I was listening to someone bring their appeal for help to the mayor of the city where she lived. Her group urgently needed some documents from a certain department of the city government and that department had verbally agreed to their request but had never given them the documents they needed. Her wording was a little unfortunate: "Please pay attention to us and give us your promise of help." The chairman was immediately irritated. He asked the speaker if she was suggesting that the city council wasn't paying attention, and reminded her impatiently that the city had already given a promise of help. The woman would have left feeling belittled except that another member of the board spoke up and thanked her for what she was doing and encouraged her to continue. The lesson could be that when we approach people who think themselves important we shouldn't try to communicate our distress but instead express much gratitude and include a little flattery.

If God were like that city council he would have given one promise to Abraham and expected Abraham to be content with that and remain confident through a long, unspecified waiting time. God is not like that. He repeated his promise to Abraham at least six times (six times that we know of) before the birth of Isaac. How nice you say; if only God would give me promises and repeat them. But God has. His word is full of promises from beginning to end. Every promise is available to you, because we are all God's chosen people. Chosen meaning that God chose us before we chose him. Even before you see the fulfillment of those promises you can appropriate them and as you do so they will begin to be fulfilled. When people read a promise in the Bible they feel that they cannot take that promise personally because God made it $o someone else. But God does not change when he works with different people. The Apostle Paul said that no scripture was meant to be a private scripture for one group only.

With the promise came instructions. First, God instructed Abraham to leave where he lived and go to a place God would show him. When he got to that place God instructed him to walk about the land that his children would inherit. We have already applied this instruction to ourselves. Firstly, God calls us to begin a new life with him, and next he encourages us to explore all the different aspects of our life with God. The third instruction is to walk before God and be perfect.

That word 'perfect' really had me worried . In my thirties, it caused me to feel guilt, failure and fear because I knew I was not, and could not, be perfect. I came into contact with a group of earnest Christians who really thought that they, but not me, were sinless. Later I realized that a person who imagines they are sinless does not understand what sin is.

Perfection when we are talking about our relationship to God means forgiveness. Because there is no other way we can be perfect. Forgiveness however is a continual requirement on our part. There is a very natural tendency to say that when we made our first confession of faith we were forgiven our sins and then to ignore any that come after that.

"Walk before me" has been interpreted as 'walk in my presence' and this is our best way of understanding the command. When we live and act in constant awareness of God's nearness we are walking in his presence. During this kind of life-style we become aware of small failures and minor inconsistencies, things we previously overlooked. Abraham's life of perfection did not mean that he had no sins but that he brought them out into his consciousness and examined them, recognizing where he needed to change and altering his behavior accordingly.

People naturally resist talking about sins. It causes anxiety. But talking about the possibility of being perfect does not frighten them. This is an age when people aspire for great things. When it is understood that perfection means recognising and changing harmful behavior, people become interested in the possibilities of uniting with God.

There is no size difference in sinfulness, which is very discouraging for morally motivated people. It puts them on the same level as criminals. No one wants that to happen, but a small break in any circuit has the same affect as a large break: the power doesn't go through.

When you were little did you ever have a Sunday School Teacher or grandparent who in their effort to control your behavior warned you, "God is watching everything you do," and writing it down in his book." Well, it's a misconstruction of a beautiful prophecy. Towards the end of the Old Testament period, the people who loved God spoke often to each other about God. God listened, says Malachi the prophet, and caused a book to be written to remember them. "These people shall be mine," he says, "in the time when I collect my valued possessions together."

These three instructions roughly correspond to stages in our spiritual development. First of all, we respond to God by stepping out into a new kind of life, a life shared with him. After we've been in this life for a little while, God encourages us to explore spiritual life, to see how many different practices and aspects there are and to have spiritual adventures. Then, as we are becoming familiar with the spiritual life comes this instruction to be always aware of God's presence and continually to subject our actions to the searchlight of his love and intelligence.

I like the way the King James Version translates it: 'Walk before me,' because in another place God says to the huge army of pilgrims, "I will go before you, but I will also be your rear guard." That's reassuring because, if we begin to be open, transparent people acting all of a piece with our hearts and our faith, we might sometimes be in danger. For instance, because we refuse to hate the people who do wicked things, we may become very unpopular with some people around us who are reveling in hatred. [I recently heard a political candidate say, "The Christians want to hug terrorists; we want to kill them."] To refuse to hate and fear may make us very unpopular, and that is why I like the translation that suggests that God is at my back as I walk before him. It's the act of terrorism I hate, not the person. I don't want to kill the terrorist. I want the terrorist to stop terrorising.

God's fourth instruction was the one that makes us shudder and we will come to that later.

When David died, I at first found being in the home we had lived in together comforted me. But after some years, I could no longer find comfort in the empty house. I asked another widow named Annabelle, how she managed, and she replied, "Well, I live with God." To walk in God's presence is to have him with us in the awful empty places but also to have him with us when our baby grandchild looks into vacant space and laughs as though she sees something or someone we cannot see. To have him with us whether everyone disapproves of us or whether everyone approves of us. It also means that we can scrutinize their disapproval or approval and ask whether it is deserved. If we have the answer in our hearts that what we have done is something that is honorable and fair, then we do not need to hide from the blazing light that shines in and around us as we walk with God.

Chapter 23

FAMILY FAILURE?
Cast out the slave woman and her son

God directed Abraham to do something many people would consider wrong. Abraham had a problem. His first wife demanded that he send away his second wife. Sarah, the first wife had given her maid Hagar to Abraham, and he had taken Hagar to be his wife. Sarah now refers to her as 'this slave'. Not only does she want to send away the slave-wife, she also wants to send away Abraham's first-born son, Ishmael, the child he had with Hagar. At one time, Sarah had wanted to make Hagar's baby her own. Now she wants him sent away.

It was a family celebration when this situation erupted. Abraham gave a great feast when his son Issac was weaned. Since babies were nursed for much longer than our customary nine months, Isaac was probably two or older when he was weaned. Looking at the ages given in the Old Testament Isaac's step-brother, and Abraham's first born son, Ishmael was fourteen when the baby was born. Something in his behavior towards the baby alarmed Sarah. It might have been that he was laughing derisively at the child. Sarah fears that the other woman's son will try to seize Isaac's inheritance. Brothers frequently kill brothers to gain an inheritance. Sarah wants it made clear that Ishmael is not the heir.

Three people are involved in this family friction: Abraham the person with the power to make decisions, Sarah the person with a position to uphold, and Hagar the person with nothing but an unwanted son. Who do you identify with as you read this account? Whose side was God on? That question is too simple. Here we have three people, all with some degree of trust in God. Would God be siding with one person against another? The language of the Bible is that God is 'for' those who trust him. That includes all three people.

Even today it seems that the worst conflicts break out during the biggest celebrations. I want to ask you, which causes the most problems? Is it the original action (the one that caused the problem in the first place) or the reaction to the problem? A wrong solution often produces more damage than the original problem. Even in a family row where only words are used, the violent speech that follows the offence is often worse than the offence itself. In tribal days, there was a clan and a chieftain to listen to the problem and offer advice. But Abraham is his own tribe and his own chieftain. Today, few families have a plan ready for the conflicts that may or may not erupt. Everyone just acts on their own advice.

It was Sarah who suggested that Abraham marry her slave, and who now suggests that he send her away. One might think that Abraham would never want to listen to anything else she had to say. Surprisingly, God directs Abraham to listen to her.. Early in the morning Abraham gives Hagar bread and a container of water and sends her out into the wilderness. So there they are: two people alone in a hot, dry desert. When the water is gone, Ishmael is weak from thirst and hunger. Hagar who is probably stronger because she had a life time of servitude behind her, lays him down and goes somewhere else so that she will not have to watch him die. Probably, Abraham knew that this would happen and considered it the safest solution. Hagar had roots in Egypt. If her son grew and flourished, he might bring a tribe to execute vengeance against Abraham and his son. Even if that didn't happen in his lifetime, there might be a threat to Isaac and his descendents for generations. Revenge motives last a long time.

God does not condemn Abraham for not waiting until he was a hundred to receive the promised child. He doesn't condemn Sarah for losing hope and finding her own solution. Out in the desert, Hagar is disregarding God's promise to her that Ishmael will be the father of a multitude. Humans are often very relieved when the promises they have made are forgotten, but God cannot dishonor himself by forgetting his promises.

The angel who speaks to Hagar tells her that God has heard the weeping of her dying son. He still hears the voices of those who weep and those who die. For the second time in her short life of faith, she sees a well and Ishmael drinks and lives. His single mother raises him alone in the desert, and eventually finds a wife for him: a woman from Egypt, her own country.

We had scornful, hostile people attending the churches I served. This was frequent among the churches who chose me for their pastor because they were from towns where the local industry has closed down or moved away. When this happens, the people who are left behind are often unable to pay off their debts or pay for health insurance. They cannot move away because depreciated values result in their owing more mortgage than they can sell the property for. When this happens some people come to church either angry or depressed and become bossy, scornful trouble-makers. When trouble erupted in the church, the governing body often expressed a wish to get rid of the trouble-makers. I had no decision-making power, but I did have the power to teach, advise and influence, so I could have complied with their wishes. David, my husband, who had been a pastor longer than I had, and who served informally as my pastor, reminded me that Jesus knew Judas was plotting against him but Jesus never tried to get rid of him. I struggled with the trouble-makers, but not against them and I never let go of them. That was my own personal understanding of how love acts. God didn't let go of Ishmael either.

Listening to the troubled families I've served and counseled, I've often been forced to admit that separating from quarrelsome relatives is better than contaminating everyone with hatred. Putting them out into today's civilized jungle with inadequate support is a very last resort however.

Why did God direct Abraham to do something so callous? There are at least two easy solutions when we come to something in scriptures (anyone's scripture) that we can't understand. One is to say that the record is mistaken. The other is to explain away the difficulty until it comes into line with our own understanding of God. I follow the example of Jesus. He accepted the scripture that he had received (at that time it was the Septuagint) in the form that his faith community had handed it down to him, and learnt from that. The other solution is to explain away the difficulty. I don't do that, because the purpose of reading scripture is to understand something beyond myself, and I would defeat that purpose if I did away with the difficulties.

Now let me talk about what I do understand, because on two points the record is so clear that I don't have to attempt to explain anything at all. First; God (says the scripture) was with the lad. That doesn't mean I can treat my relatives badly because God is with them. But look at this recorded fact. Here is the rejected son of a rejected woman, without a hope in the wilderness, and God is with him. Second, God blesses Ishmael as well as Abraham. Previously, Abraham, unable to believe that Sarah could have a child at the age of ninety, had asked God to accept Ishmael as Abraham's heir. God said, "No", and continued to promise that Abraham's heir would be born from his first wife Sarah, the woman who had loyally accompanied Abraham on his journey. Abraham seems quite willing to forget Sarah's own hopes but God will not. God refuses to grant Abraham's request but assures him that he has heard it and promises that he will bless Ishmael also, and make of him also a great nation. Ishmael, like Abraham and Sarah, like you and me is blessed to be a blessing. God will make Ishmael into more than Ishmael could have made himself.

A major characteristic of all three monotheistic religions is that all of them make mistakes. A human characteristic is that we do wrong while we are trying to do right. A comfort to Abraham and to us, is that God takes care of the mistakes we have made. Perhaps I am not the only old person who looks back at my life and worries about the mistakes I made but never intended. One of the serenities of old age is watching God repairing those mistakes. An excitement (oh how the old long for excitement) is that now, more than ever before, all three religions spend time and effort studying how to do the right they intended and not the harm they never intended. There is hope.

God's covenant with Abraham was for the purpose that he might reveal himself to all the people yet to be born by showing them how he kept faith with Abraham. By looking at Abraham's life, we see God's self-revelation. By displaying his mercy, grace and love, God commends himself to us, showing us that we can trust him. That is why I say that faith is a gift. God is giving us the evidence we need to trust him.

When Abraham died at the age of one hundred and seventy-five, his sons Isaac and Ishmael buried him. So, somewhere along the line, there had been some sort of reconciliation. Working towards reconciliation often becomes one of the major tasks of old age.

Lacking all other resources, Ishmael became an expert with the bow and arrow, and fathered twelve sons, all of them princes of their tribe. He roamed free wherever he chose, never subjugated, never subdued. In time, his descendents would have their own prophet and develop their own religion. But never their own God – no one has that.

In Abraham's lifetime, God was demonstrating not only his own nature but the nature of his blessing. The blessing is never divided, but always multiplied.

Chapter 24

THE AWFUL AWFUL THING
God tested Abraham

W e took our sons to visit underground caves in Derbyshire, England. Hanging from the roof of the caves were long, icicle-shaped mineral deposits called stalactites. They reflected the light of the guide's flashlight. On level places, similarly tapered stalagmites rose up from the floor of the cave to meet them. Silent, dark and beautiful, the caves were a kind of sub-terranean temple, revealed only when a shaft of light illuminated them.

I couldn't appreciate the beauty because I was too afraid one of my beloved sons would fall through the cracks in the floor of the cave. The depth of the fissures had never been measured because they twisted and narrowed, but people had been stuck in the narrow places, and some had been lost forever when they fell through a wide fissure into the waters of an underground river. On the way out we were each given a long stalactite, beautiful and fragile. One of our party just had to test how fragile it was, and this thing of age and beauty snapped in his fingers. Does God do things like that? Did he test the most beautiful person alive to see if he'd break?

The Bible clearly says that God tested Abraham by commanding him to offer his son Isaac as a burnt offering. Bible readers shudder when they come to this part of their scriptures. People reading the Bible for the first time close the book and put it away.

God tested Abraham. We can understand that circumstances, such as a war, or evil people, or a wicked king, test our obedience to God, but does God need to do it himself? Also, while we're regarding this sentence with horror we wonder why God needed to test anything. Surely he knew without testing. In later years King David would say that God continually sees us and even knows what we are going to say before we say it. So why did God test Abraham? One reason might have been that Abraham himself needed to know. There is something constructive about knowing what is our ability to withstand any trial and something creative in knowing where we need to do to grow stronger. Some people can look back on their lives and say, "On that occasion I did not fail God even though the trial was hard." This is not boasting you understand but recognizing that temptations overcome make us stronger. God is strengthening every one who believes in him so that he can bless them and they can become a source of blessing.

In this respect, Abraham's obedience has become a source of blessing to all who believe in the One God. The account can be mined again and again for lessons specific to each individual's circumstances and trials.

The outstanding blessing of this story is that the God of Abraham is shown, forever after, as not requiring child sacrifice. When Moses lead the descendents of Abraham back to the land that Abraham had lived in, he assembled them and declared that God would be angry if they followed the local custom and offered their children as sacrifice. Some of them did not follow his instructions. They had a choice of gods in that land, so if Abraham's God did not grant their request for fertile farm and family, they began instead to pray to the local gods. When these gods did not immediately respond their priests said they must be placated with greater offerings, and what greater offering could there be than the first-born child? The prophet Jeremiah tells the people (who were not listening anyhow) that they had forsaken the God of Abraham and profaned their country by burning their children in the fire as an offering to the god Baal. Two of the kings of Israel, Ahaz and Ahab, sought victory and wealth for their nation by making their sons and daughters burnt offerings to the god Molech. When he is reproaching the people for building altars in high places to sacrifice their sons and daughters to Molech, Jeremiah says that God did not command or consider such an action. God called it an abomination. Words are never enough to convince us not to act in a certain way, especially if 'everyone else' is doing it; we need an example. The example was that when Abraham had bound his son and fastened his to the place of fire the angel of God called out of heaven and said, "Do not harm the boy."

What God knows, as C.S.Lewis tells us, is more important than what we know. God says to Abraham, "Now I know." What did he know? That Abraham feared God. In the sacred records orally rehearsed, written, preserved and collated for us by generations of people who feared God, the word 'fear' means to honor and respect with great care. God does not act alone. He involves people in his actions. We are being the people of God, not just his subjects. Perhaps it was essential for the test to be carried out so that Abraham could know what God knew. Or perhaps it was so that, for ever after, this story would be one of the greatest explanations of the relationship between the worshiper and worshiped. God desires obedience more than offerings. Obedience was the gift that Abraham gave to God that day. Obedience, meaning conformity to the will of God is the gift that God sought from Abraham and seeks from us. God is not willing that anyone should perish but that we should all come to him and be blessed.

Abraham's obedience was not blind, and his faith was not unreasonable. In the much-loved church where I grew up we would sing songs with titles like, "Only believe" or tell the people we hoped to convince that all that God required was that they believe. We didn't give them a lot of time to reason. We didn't give them a lot of evidence to convince them. When the invitation had been offered and refused, we considered them 'lost', although no one is lost while they live. Abraham's obedience that day was the result of faith, and his faith was the result of the evidence of God's activity in his life.

The evidence of God's activity showed itself as protection, provision and promises fulfilled. Abraham's household was orderly, and his servants respected him. Abraham acted with generous fairness and refused to be indebted to anyone. He was rich because at that time people saw riches as evidence of God's pleasure. Such earthly things showed the activity of the divine in the life of Abraham.

A man, or woman, deeply reverent of all things Jewish, wrote to the Christian Jews that Abraham expected to receive his son back from the dead after he made a sacrifice of him. He or she probably deduced that from the words of Abraham when he left the servants at the foot of the hill, and told them, "The lad and I will go and worship, and we will return."

It was also evident to that writer that Abraham would remember God's statement that Isaac was the particular son through whom the blessing of God would be granted to all the nations of the earth. Abraham would also remember that, when he doubted his ability to have a son by Sarah, God had said to him, "Is anything too hard for the Lord?" Knowing that Isaac was the son he had been granted after years of promise, he believed that God would make Isaac live again, even though dead. This first faint understanding of the resurrection of the dead was based on reason. A greater demonstration was to follow but not for hundreds of years.

Abraham and Isaac made a burnt offering of a ram which had got tangled in a bush and was easy to catch. Together they returned to the servants waiting at the foot of the hill and went home to Sarah, who, knowing the local customs, may have been tormented by her own guesses. On the way they passed under a tree that Abraham had planted. It was under this tree that Abraham made a practice of calling on the Only God. Abraham had named the tree, 'God is eternal.'

There is a verse in the New Testament which frightened me when I was young and ardent. Paul the Apostle instructs us to offer ourselves as living sacrifices. I thought this meant I had to voluntarily suffer hardship. My friends and I tried to do this, depriving ourselves of sleep and not eating things we liked. (It was wartime so that part was easy.) The effort didn't produce godliness, piety or holiness in us, although I understand that for some people it does. Actually, "sacrifice" and "worship" meant the same thing in the language used at that time, so what Paul meant was that people who trust God are to be continually worshiping God in actions and thoughts throughout the day. This is practiced by followers of God in all three monotheistic religions.

Although God and Abraham had demonstrated that God does not require human sacrifice, a lot of leaders, priests and prophets have become rather good at requiring it since that time. They do not require the faithful to be physically sacrificed, but they demand other kinds of sacrifice: priests shall not marry, women shall not work outside the home, and youths will obey every demand of their nation whether it is just or not. Some leaders have become very powerful by sacrificing other people instead of themselves.

rificing other people instead of themselves.

Christians have particular reverence for the story of Abraham preparing to sacrifice his son because they see in it a similarity to the death of Jesus. But Jesus was not killed by his father; he was executed by people. Obedience killed Jesus because he continued to do what he had been sent to do in the face of powerful opposition. He had been sent from God with a message, and like the prophets before him, the message was despised and the only way to silence him was to execute him. This time there was no angel saying, "Do not harm." God had other plans. There is however a difference from all the prophets that came before: Jesus had come into the world to do the will of God and he had not strayed from that purpose, neither had he failed God in any way, not even once. God therefore gave life to the corpse. Jesus came out of the burial cave and went to visit his followers. After spending forty days with them, telling them the good news of the Kingdom of Heaven, he went to be with his Father in Heaven and was not seen again, except in visions.

Many of Abraham's descendents saw in Jesus a similarity to the animal sacrifices they had made to cleanse themselves from sin. Jesus understood his death in this way. He understood that the death of one completely obedient individual could be credited to many people to take away their sins. Animal sacrifices were no longer needed. One person had died for all people for all time.

There had been a promise that the children of Abraham were waiting for, a promise about a new heart. The promise was given to the prophets Isaiah and Jeremiah at a time when God was being despised by the people. Because God will not give up the humanity that he has brought into being, he had new plans. Now that humans could see by their own demonstration that they needed God in order to be truly human, and not like wild animals fighting and tearing and consuming each other, he would give them a new heart, and a new spirit. With that new heart and new spirit, they would desire to do what God required. What does God require? "To do justice, love kindness and walk humbly with God." When Jesus walked out of the burial cave that day, the promise happened. Everyone who believed him became changed. They lost their indifference to God and became eager to please him. Their joy now was to do the will of God. God had given his people a new heart and put a right spirit within them. The new heart was not confined to the blessed children of Abraham but to all people everywhere.

Many people who are not blood descendants of Abraham and his twelve great, great, grandsons claim to be children of Abraham by faith. They have believed that Jesus is God with us. God has credited them with the obedience of Jesus and they are now Jews by faith. The Jews are somewhat shocked and indignant that people they call heathens have lined up as children of Abraham, but the Jews recognize that God is gracious and does not reward us on the basis of who we are but on who we trust. Once again the blessing has multiplied.

Chapter 25

SEEING THE BLESSING

Isaac found comfort

God's self-revelation produces man's self-understanding. One of the great serenities of old age is that we know who we are.

Satisfaction is another serenity of old age. Most of us can look back over our lives and realize that we've carried out most of our intentions, achieved more than we expected, and been given the fulfillment of many hopes. I'm a very average person with only a small measure of achievement and yet I am amazed that I can look out at life, as it is lived in my town, and say, 'Whatever it is; I've done it, had it, and got it.' Amazing. Especially when I haven't been particularly energetic or wise. I never knew this until I got old. Before that I was often blind to blessings because I was continually driven by financial needs and worthy ambitions.

Abraham had traveled through three major urban centers, and knew the places in between. He had been the rich husband of a beautiful wife. He had been generous to his relative and respected by his servants. He had done things he was ashamed of and things he was proud of. Kings had made covenants with him, but he had never lost his independence. He had known famine and feasting, dug wells and provided hospitality. May you be so blessed.

Sarah died. Abraham's half sister, his wife, and mother of his promised child died before he was even near the end of his own life. Sarah was one hundred and twenty seven years old when she died. At that time Abraham was one hundred and thirty seven. He would live another thirty-eight years. Isaac was thirty-seven when his mother died, forty when he married and sixty when his twin sons were born. For the last fifteen years of his life, Abraham had the joy of watching his grandchildren grow.

We would perhaps say of Sarah that she had had a hard life, leaving the relative comforts of the cities for the tents and travels of a nomad, and being despised by everyone because she was infertile. However, she escaped what most wives dread most of all: she never became a widow. Abraham made his first purchase of land and buried her in a cave on land he had bought from the Hitite tribe.

Abraham married again and had six more sons but gave them gifts and sent them away when they were old enough. Only Isaac was the son through whom God's long slow process of self-revelation and consequent blessing would come.

We do not know what was carved over the burial cave to identify it as Sarah's, but her epitaph has lasted as long as the Bible. The record says that Isaac needed comforting after her death. When all our living has ended, this is the monument we most hope for: to have lived so that we are missed when we are gone. Abraham's trusted servant found a wife for him of the same family as Isaac's mother and father. We watch her, as we read the record, making the long journey to the home of her unseen husband and when she is almost there, seeing the dim outline of a solitary person walking towards her. She veils herself and goes towards him. Isaac takes her into his mother's tent. She becomes his wife and he loves her. He is, says the record, comforted after his mother's death.

Love. You would have expected that word to be in the first chapter of the first part of the history of mankind. It doesn't come until the twenty-second chapter where we are told that Abraham loved Isaac. It comes again when Isaac loves his wife. Strange that the word we use so frequently now took so long to appear.

Through Abraham and his descendents we come to understand God a little. He is too remote and too different from us for us to ever understand him completely. Through the long history of Abraham's descendents we learn that love and righteousness, accompanied by grace and mercy, are the characteristics he has chosen to demonstrate to us so that we may know him. The knowledge is not academic but experiential.

Blessing is shown to be the activity of God upon our lives and God's intention is not only that we should know him, but that we should become like him, so that the image of God in which he made humanity should become stronger and clearer. Ultimately, blessing means being made in God's likeness.

May the blessing of God be on you, may your blessings multiply, and may you become a blessing to many.

End Notes

Where I have quoted the Bible it has been a loose quotation giving the meaning but not the exact words.

But read for yourself:

The story of Abraham and Sarah - Genesis chapters 11 – 25.

Be fruitful and multiply - Geneses 1 verse 22

Abraham rejoices to see my day - John 8 verse 56

Abraham believed God and the Lord reckoned - Genesis 15 verse 6.

Faith was reckoned to Abraham for righteousness - Romans 4.13.

What does the Lord require? Micah 6.verse 8.

One might say that Levi paid tithes - Hebrews 7 verse 9.

In the image of God he created them - Genesis 1.28.

The faith of Abraham - Hebrews 11 verses 1- 17.

A single sacrifice for all sins for all time - Hebrews 10 verse 11.

The Lord bless you and keep you - Numbers 6 verses 22 – 27.

The faithful will abound with blessings - Proverbs 28 verse 20.

I will put a new spirit within you - Ezekiel 11 verse 19.

I will give you a new heart Ezekiel - 36 verses 26 & 27

I have used STRONG'S HEBREW AND GREEK DICTIONARIES by James Strong, published by Hodder and Stoughton Limited, London EC4 and THE ILLUSTRATED BIBLE DICTIONARY published by Inter-Varsity Press and Tyndale, and Hodder and Stoughton.

C.S. Lewis talks about being known by God in his book THE WEIGHT OF GLORY

God .. is not willing that any should perish – 2 peter chapter 3 verse 9

Thanks

To my sons Paul and Philip for suggesting and helping with this book.

To my daughter-in-law Robyn who encouraged me.

To Robyn's parents who read my blog and suggested I turn it into a book.

To my friend and co-worker Pastor Scott Keeble who also read my blog and said that if I wrote a book he would buy it. Here you are Scott.

Many, many thanks to my editor Paul Hine, who has put a lot of time and effort into helping me collate scattered chapters and bring some shape into this small book.

Printed in the United States
106292LV00004B/376-399/A

9 781432 716998